I DON'T KNOW

There are times when the pen moves
    by itself
And there are times when I am so inspired
    I can't hold the pen
When I have to jump around
    to reassure the ground

A JOHN MACRAE BOOK

HENRY HOLT AND COMPANY NEW YORK

BOB HOLMAN'S

...

THE COLLECT CALL OF THE WILD

Henry Holt and Company, Inc.
Publishers since 1866
115 West 18th Street
New York, New York 10011

Henry Holt® is a registered
trademark of Henry Holt and Company, Inc.

Published in Canada by Fitzhenry & Whiteside Ltd.,
195 Allstate Parkway, Markham, Ontario L3R 4T8.

Library of Congress Cataloging-in-Publication Data
Holman, Bob.
[Collect call of the wild]
Bob Holman's the collect call of the wild.—1st ed.
p.   cm.
"A John Macrae book."
I. Title.
PS3558.035588065   1995   94-24221
811'.54—dc20   CIP
ISBN 0-8050-3674-1
ISBN 0-8050-3672-5 (An Owl Book: pbk.)

Henry Holt books are available for special
promotions and premiums. For details contact:
Director, Special Markets.

First Edition—1995

Designed by Paula R. Szafranski

Printed in the United States of America
All first editions are printed on acid-free paper.∞

1 3 5 7 9 10 8 6 4 2
1 3 5 7 9 10 8 6 4 2
(pbk.)

To the Citizens of the United States of Poetry,
please accept the charges!

CONTENTS

A rule is used to indicate a space between stanzas of a poem wherever such spaces are lost in pagination.

ACKNOWLEDGMENTS

The inspiration for this book came from Mike Tyler.

Special thanks also to Miguel Algarín, Cathy Bowman, Hal Sirowitz, and CD Wright, who helped put it together.

And to Jack Macrae who saw it through.

Some of these poems have appeared in previous books: *Tear To Open (This This This This This This)*, Power Mad Press, Barb Barg; *Panic*DJ!*, University Arts Resources, Daryl Chin and Larry Qualls; *Cupid's Cashbox*, Jordan Davies Books; *Eight Chinese Poems* and *SWEAT&SEX&POLITICS!*, PeKa Boo Press, Eric and Rebecca Edwards.

Poems have also appeared via audio: "ROCK'N'ROLL MYTHOLOGY," *Words on 45*, Vito Ricci and Ann Rower; "SWEAT&SEX&POLITICS" and "THE IMPOSSIBLE RAP," Panic*DJ! Prods.; *Sugar, Alcohol and Meat*, Giorno Poetry Systems, John Giorno; *Live from the Knitting Factory Vol. IV* and *Nuyorican Symphony*, Knitting Factory/Atlantic, Michael Dorf, Paul Skiff and Carolyn Peyser. On video: *Rapp It Up!*, Manhattan Poetry Video Project, Rose Lesniak; *Poetry Spots*, Dave Shore, WNYC-TV; *Words in Your Face*, Alive TV/PBS, Josh Blum and Mark Pellington; and "MTV Spoken Word: Unplugged," Robert Small.

Among the magazines and anthologies where these poems have appeared (with apologies to those not listed): *ABC No Rio Dinero*, Josh Gosciak; *Ahnoi*, Joel Lewis; *Aloud: Voices from the Nuyorican Poets Café* (Henry Holt and Co.); *Baltimore City Paper*; *Barney*, Jack Skelley; *Big Wednesday*, Betsy Lerner; *Bomb*, Betsy Sussler; *Bombay Gin*, John Wright; *Brooklyn Review*, Jeffery Conway; *The Cheap Review*; *Cocodrilo*, David Cameron; *Colorado North Review*; *Contact II*, Maurice Kenny; *Cover*, Jeff Wright; *Dis*, Adrienne Laban; *The East Village Eye*, Leonard Schwartz; *Exquisite Corpse*, Laura Rosenthal; *Framework*, Roberto Bedoya; *The Fuse*; *Gandahba*, Tom Savage; *A Gathering of the Tribes*; *Giants Play Well in the*

Drizzle, Martha King; *Kameleon,* Joe Speer; *The Ledge,* Timothy Monaghan; *Literati Internazionale,* Eugene B. Redmond; *Long News in the Short Century,* Barbara Henning; *Long Shot,* Nancy Mercado, Danny Shot, and Eliot Katz; *Mag City,* Michael Scholnick and Greg Masters; *Make Room for Dada,* Claire McMahon; *Malandragem,* Sol Gaitan; *Milk Quarterly,* Ravi Singh; *Nashville's Poetry Newsletter*; *The National Poetry Magazine of the Lower East Side,* Ron Kolm; *New American Writing,* Maxine Chernoff and Paul Hoover; *New Censorship,* Ivan Zuvanjieff; *Out of This World* (Crown), Anne Waldman; *Peau Sensible,* Buddy Kold; *Pinched Nerves,* Ken DiMaggio; *The Poetry Flash,* Joyce Jenkins and Richard Silberg; *The Poetry Project Newsletter*; *Rant,* Alfred Vitale; *Scarlet,* Alice Notley and Douglas Oliver; *Shell*; *Southpaw,* George and Chris Tysh; *Talisman,* Ed Foster; *Teachers and Writers Handbook of Poetic Forms* (Teachers & Writers Press) Ron Padgett; *Telephone,* Maureen Owen; *Transfer,* Gary Lenhart; *Up Late,* (4 Walls 8 Windows) Andrei Codrescu; *Wail,* Neal and Kerry Zagerella; *Woodland Pattern,* Ann Kingsbury and Karl Gartung; *The World,* Charlotte Carter, Tony Towle, and Lewis Warsh. *¡Holas y gracias!* to the Nuyorican Poets, Nation of Slam, St. Mark's Poetry Projectiles, Cowboy Poets Gathering in Elko, ASL Poets, Washington Square Films, Nuyo Records . . .

And to Elizabeth, Dakota, Sophie, and Daisy—the last word is love.

BOB
HOLMAN'S

...

THE
COLLECT
CALL OF THE
WILD

1

TEAR TO OPEN
(THIS THIS THIS THIS THIS THIS)

(   )

Go ahead
Open the door
Hello white water
Hello there bridge
Hello figure
On the other
Side of the bridge
Saying hello
Just myself

Who Knows

Who cares
Why bother
How come
What possible difference
Could it make

The Garage

I fix the spot
Every time
I put my foot down

1

When I lift it
I leave it
I return
To fix it
Thank you
Very much

Sad Song

You can cry now
This is a sad song
Out the window
Over the miles
Look, it's your hometown!
This look is your return
Even though nobody's home.
Some return. Some river
With no boat.
Don't tell me about it.
Don't tell anyone.

Sailing Back Capital

after Chan Fang-sheng

You've got a million feet
Why do you stand on your head?
Your pockets still fall down
My salary plunks to the ground.
Why is my head white sand?
New poems all of a sudden.

2

The Return

I am standing in the doorway.
I have put my suitcase down.
You are staring at me strangely
Because I am a high school manikin
And you are my steady dresser.

Help

Here—you drink, I'll write.
The sun's going down. We won't be
      needing it anymore,
So let's tape these blossoms back on this tree.
The branches waving their naked arms, "Help! Help!"
Hey!
Hold the ladder steady, you!
"Help! Help!"

After Ch'in Kuan

Look at that!
Too bad.

I love strong grass up here
And the trees down there.

I cannot bear the churring of the night-jar.
Throw your gum away.

Rain has struck the pear blossom!

Out of work?
Lock the door.

So Far Away

It is dawn and the bouffant is dragging.
Paint, paint that eye. It is history
That makes you paint them so far away.
So sad. So natural to feel that sadness.
The little smile in the little frown.

Previously Saving

You no think me
You no love me
This old custom
Break heart
Folk custom
Way-things-used-to-be
Previously saving each other
We think go ho ho
So difficult, loyalty
Like white heads
Disappearing in white water

He Refuses to Enter the Marketplace Even to Buy Prestige

Putt putt little cafique
She puts her hands on your shoulders
And pushes herself up to dive from them
Pushing you down where you see
The clearest you ever saw

Dreaming

All day to watch this petal fall
    Two to one it doesn't
        It doesn't

Secretly the evening steals
    Spring and the cow

I thought the curtains would answer
    I thought I'd get the money
        And buy the whole garden

Singing in the garden
        As the petal deliriously falls
    And settles on your breast
        Where your breast would be

I will not wake up
    No matter what
        To see how it ends

Rain

for Danny O'Neil

How I love
To stand
In the driving rain
Blowing my horn
At the entrance
To the Holland Tunnel

Saying Goodby

Now you're giving wine to the horse!
Why did I ever ask *you* for directions?
You ask *me* why I asked *you?*
Who's the guide around here anyway?
Surely we're not lost.
Are we lost?
We're lost.
Let us never go back
May we never be found.

Is

What is is time
What the arrow points to
The hole in the arrow
To fill the belly time
The fork to the mouth
It is dinner time
It is time to eat
It is time to eat time

Here's an Example

We could sail away
We could fall through
        The ventilator slats in the floor
Every word is important
You are a poet
Talking to a painting, learning all
Over again how a white street

6

Can lead night around the side
Where love is the horizon
Where the cup has two handles

What It Is

More than you know me there is
        Something in my eye. Is it
A volcano? I mean window. I mean,
Excuse me, are you talking to me?
I brought you something, but you
Came through it so at least everything
Will be different, starting immediately.
Difficulty is your daughter, too, she adds.
Vast apples! How sorry the sorry image,
Romanticism cubed. That is the question:
Forget it! Now, slowly remove propeller
From tuba, gently stretching umbilical
Accordion to full spectrum—that's it.
Your move. Your witness. Yours truly.

Long Hoe, Long Hoe with Your Raw Wooden Handle

All the way to the groundline
And then up comes the shoot
Except now with yam eyes in my pocket
And the snow around you, Long Hoe
I must sit and think of my family hunger
And will return either emptyhanded
Or offering the seeds that would harvest fill
And this is the second time I have sung this

Up All Night

And it's still night
But there's a bird
Flying into it
Taking its share

All I do is sit here
And write poems

Do City Morning

Awake watermelon my eyes
Door to door. The sun is investigating.
We don't mind, we are coffee.
Wires spread, pinching blue so blue.
Clocks growl, radios sputter.
Do people wearing no faces yet
Sigh magic n a crease n a jog
Footwork my life as an individual
By King of the Bees a narrative
Enclosing this city sea of air
God's dirigibles' war cries & sensitives
These headlines across morning's table
To the dead giveaway of your hands.

Thinking of Li Po

a millennium or so after Tu Fu

An imperishable fame of 1,000 years
Is but a paltry afterlife affair
What time is it?

Singing in the rain
   I think I'll talk about
      How difficult it all is
Lying here in bed
   Writing with you asleep
      On my shoulder

After Li Po

No oar but this magnolia
No boat but this spicewood
Carve a jade flute, make it gold
Make it beautiful as this bottle of wine
Make the bottle a woman
Make me a king on an empty hill
I'm so full of wine and poetry
Laughing, my pen falls down,
Ending this poem

Now it can bring me wealth and fame!

Sung to the Tune of "The Weary Road"

Being served the best wine in a gold cup
While the musicians unstrap their instruments
   From jade & tortoise cases
Seven varieties of hibiscus
   On a feathered curtain
The thick quilt depicts nine kinds of grapes. . . .
I'm getting old
People have begun to listen to me

They think everybody always did
Well, now that I have your attention
Here's a song to the tune of "The Weary Road"

Center Field

"Judge, I was just singing and thought I was in the shower. Came down so slow and easy, how was I to know it was a grapefruit? Fly? Certain of the lee! O, they shout, if only we could cover his eyes and stand him back against the wall, where he belongs, aim our bats in that fat territory—he's but a line to guard it, anyway. I vacuum sound in my wide abyss. Ah, the shepherd lets nary a ball out his reach. I nod at Homers passing. Equals. Grace strength."

First Base

"Lean and rangy my clumsy hulk tacks for bloopers, bellows takeoff at bunts. I am that first step, sack on the line. My claw stretches and retracts. Can't put off my bulk turf protection—my bod to fill the chinks in this primary quadrant, a block down the line. Hiss reach. Breach the space stretch as the enemy pours it on. Huffer. *Shit.* My one-on-one if he's so-called safe, if he's on it. He crab, titillatingly a-flutter vs. the sacred sackguard of me. I'll hook 'em, Pick off, fave play. My southpaw mores, webbed monster mitt—Boys, leave your spikes for me to ferry you, no stop payment, buck stops here, Charon me no home. No more. Hiss."

Third Base

"Let cool breeze in this torrid quarter lull you, valiant Sir, mint tea distilled to sleep. Let this be your comfortable station. Your way is laid. The last of the chalk scrapes, spikes on slate. Hey hey no need to think now, Sweetheart. Don't squeeze, where's your cough and manliness? Is this any way I let you stay as long's you like, Mister. Identify the terribly normal insects. I don't mind. It's as close as your welcome home. Where the book says you cannot go again. And I'm just quoting."

Catcher

". . . tooled ignorance. They think I'm a goddamn machine, encased, enarmored. Plug me in. Am now receiving your pitches now please follow my signals. Can catch anything _____ can throw. Sheesh. Gotta eat more leather milkshakes, my biocomputer's blinking err on the blink? On my shoulder sits el Judge, hizzoner. My crouch the pepper box. Allow me to define the confines, fading waving invisible shield solid block of air strike zone. Steam director roller, haul all into this cage."

Left Field

"When the weaker hitters come up I sort of let myself chill, stare at my feet till the grass—rough outfield grass, not infield putting green—turns purple. I'm confident with bat radar—can move on sound alone, can sense ball in wind shifts, crowd shifts. Glove up. Special delivery and right on target.
"Welcome home egg bullet."

Shortstop

"Thin think. Hot stuff. Thin reeds. Clarinet: upper register. Español. Darters. I am my toes. On 'em. Rear spikes unmuddied, who dances.

11

Toothpick scratchers. Man you try hit the hole man got you covered man on the double man—hold. Both feet on brake and accelerator. Rabbit jack. Handle, you got the skimmer's handle. My glove: braided whip. My hands: starter stoppers. Here! Here!

"Here, Ventriloquist, I throw my voice."

Luther Winslow, Second Base

Big parade
statue being carried down street
people cheering etc
green and yellow pom poms
people shout Winslow Luther, Winslow Luther
was hometown politician o early Times
they loved him
course they sorta didn't remember exickly what he look like
what they don't know or don't care, to know
statue is actually for Luther Winslow, Luther Winslow
also hometown boy but played baseball in majors
incredible 2 baseman frog legs leap frog frog
jump hump Texas Leggers bandy that about—a clove. The bolt of the
infield (not to be confused with shortstop, bolt of the infield) . . .
still, he shades towards 2nd and shallow center balls are his . . . (1st
base = belt of the infield) . . . driving the herd into the Ox Temple . . .
(3rd is the bell of the infield) . . . chokes up on thick-handled bat,
wears red (or blue) longsleeved sweatshirt under uniform, especially
visiting grays . . . (2nd base is the boil of the infield)

they thought Luther did something bad—
hung out with gamblers or married too young
or didn't marry but just lived with a dumdedumdum—a man

so everybody hailed Winslow Luther, Winslow Luther
but Luther Winslow felt proud just the same
because he was hearing his name in refrain

except for one thing.
no one noticed Luther
because the statue didn't look like Luther
it looked like Winslow

Pitcher

"How perfectly clean I long to be!

"The owner of the rubber plantation. Shrugging signs. Rotating seams. On the rub. On the mound. My individual whirlwind, tra. Pass, cross, body hurl, ballet la.

"O pawn warriors, face your numbers into the sun. There is an army out here against your one. Out here hajira, to get it over and over with. Home's not connected, Breezer. Or the edge/you see it away, ha! Slides curves steered tight, Corner Nib! My duplicity your weakness. The wind up. I say now."

Right Field

"Of course I'm last. Guess who's in the corner, yeah, the little guy. Hermit in the rough. Weighs a tad too much. A locomotive huffer chasing loopers. Cute li'l dance step takin' it on the first hop right at the knees and then the flat-gloved flip to the 2 baseman, who whirls and fires it back to first—caught in a rundown I slide and the throw hits me and I'm safe and like I've always expected it rolling the pants up under the socks, knocking the dust off, adjusting the cap."

Manager

Barks out his instructions. "First be a dog. Lie on your back and get you stomach primed. Hungry for the horse. Paw hid in claw. Voracious. Shout 'Aw c'mon, Clancy' at the bastid in blue. He's one 60's don't double in 90's, o-rig-i-nal. Cheeeee. Geometry—triangles in diamonds. Gotta take a breath gotta get a short stop tee hee. Heart-to-heart phone from the bullpen. Ah, the night's angelic. Those blinding spots are stars that blind spot the stars. May I sit down here?"

2

CUPID'S CASHBOX

Cupid's Cashbox

Mutual disenchantment was setting in!
As if water would dissolve love like
Paper—& what is paper, Love? What is
Under your hat. Guess the riddle which is
Never snuffed out so that it may burn
Longer: Happiness is mortal.

I want to be your girlfriend.

The Reader's egotism demands that emotion be served,
Not second helpings of wit. Already the water has begun
To lift ink from the page, turning it into weak
Ink, black water, blank page. Sure I know smelling
& thinking are the same thing, but as some brilliant
Critic once croaked, "What does it mean?" It means
Exasperation, a goat on a well searching for a fig leaf.
You can believe it in the morning
Even as you cry yourself to sleep at night.
You can write it all down
But the words are all made up
As lovers do, continually. . . .

How sweet the jasmine in the blue evening!
Much too sweet, it is true, under this bitter moon.

Ebbtide is rushing in as we sit on the dock of the bay,
Having forgotten how to swim. We know. We know it all.
We know up, we know down, we just don't know which is
Which anymore. That is the noon whistle, I mean the fire
Engine's siren. I say, even the cicadas take a break.

Indeed, I know what love is.
It is no secret, but you must
Forget it as I have to pass it
On. She read my future in ant hills.
I wrote a novel in the ashtray. In
It the world was ashes, but the ashes
Could grow. You could burn them, they
Would turn into trees which never stop
Growing. Trees are people, too. They watch
Our every move. They have roots. They appreciate
A nice rain. Uncomplaining. They know how to
Say goodby. When we die, trees grow
From our hearts. Burning. Turning to ashes.

Poetry

I have always liked being alone
Although I always find it hard to leave
As a matter of fact I can't
Stop thinking of you now

Elegant Study

I shall shut myself up
In my elegant study

My Shirt

I like to put it on
My arms get long that way

The Paintings Were Interesting

YES, FOLKS, it is a first!
The paintings were more interesting
Than the clothes of the hordes who
Stood in front of them at "last night's"
Opening. He who "last week" poured
Drinky-wink down her gown "that
Night" met his comeuppance in the
Form of
         A rock sat quietly the whole time
History crept. Smoke gets in your
Mouth—is someone giving you the hotfoot?
The joke is so funny I forget to eke
Out a living for my wife & children.

Fortune into a Bargain

He had a face
like a sieve.

Her love differed
from tumultuous passion

as the flowers of the field
from the splendor of a garden bed.

How pitiless are the laws of society!

Sure, a sunset is a *great* subject
for poetry—BUT is not one ridiculous
describing it in high-sounding words
before a materially-minded audience?

Awaiting the Return of the Drunk with a Broom

In time, the light of passion returned to his eyes,
And then, suddenly, it was genius or burst!
He'd been dogged by self-mistrust, earnest & true,
What's the matter with you? Now visions
Stayed put, he could look & talk at the
Same time, he could see through & through it.
His anger at the fools who looked first
At the signature, then at the work—he'd show
'Em! He began sweeping with a vengeance.
It all came back, so very clear, rushing
Towards him! He turned his back as the wave
Broke over him, & swept him out to sea.
Draw this, he said. Draw this poem, I ordered.

What a drama! Harder than walking on water, even,
It was more loved than lovely, something
You can only write down, never endure. Oh,
She uttered, as he rolled over her, fuck me now!
People actually talk like this.
He was inside the painting at the time.

Give Everyone a Drink Before We All End Up Like Bernard Shaw

"People drink because they need to stop
            being uptight assholes every once in a while

Maybe I should say like once a day

They can't pass the refrigerator without opening it, either

And once opened, not to take something would reduce the action to a symbol, a "gesture" gesture

Or Brecht ("gestus"), there was a guy, wrote and wrote, drank, indulged, traveled with a hot entourage, wives all over the place

I was there the night Dylan Thomas peed on the audience.

       I want you to know, he missed.

Excuse me, I have to go drink a beer.

Burp.

There is a jack hammering my ear. Take me at face value.

       Drop everything and come with me. Do nothing till
       you hear of me. Pass people by, give them the old
       nod, but be thinking always:

HAVE A DRINK OR YOU'RE BERNARD SHAW!"

Chaucer sighed. What a long hard day it's been. Got up,

got out of bed, dragged a comb across his head. Good morning, good morning, good morning, he called to his roommates three. One for his money, two for his show, three to get ready. . . .

Ashbery

All we can say is congratulations

When we meet him on the street

From the Jacket Blurb of a Minor Novel by a Well-Known and Respected 19th-Century French Novelist

"In scarcely any other
of his writings has

---

revealed so much of

his own inner life—
of his failures
and disappointments."

Not to mention
the day he awoke
and for no good reason
was happy.

Balzac

Mr. Balzac would like you
To finish his book
So he can go out dancing

Gotta Get My I in Shape

More differentiation!
A cave!
All you can see is black (hee hee).
The wind appears
To soothe the hillside, to titillate
The grasses. Green passes by this cave.
Beware!

I am trying desperately to get my I in shape.
But everything is going on forever out my whatever
Loving liberally and fucking literally. Blue.
Not content to translate inside news of you
To you as chance tunes noisy progress.

We've been traveling in circles
Which is fine
Because they're all the right circles

I in conclusion
            I end
With a spin

The Essence Not the Mode

Heaving stones into the sea. Ships & boats.
Rocks & stones. These are a few of my favorite
Things. Things which are themselves in the center
Of things. In the center of language. Between
"m" & "n." The "&" between. You "&" me in bed, fitting
Our arm around our head while the flower buds, would
You look at that, & blossoms glorious, wilts & dies,
Dries, & is preserved. Two water glasses on the windowsill:
Two skulls. My fingers in your mouth, your love in mine—
You can taste the good old classical mode as it fits

Shapely over the wild vines on the wall we cling to.
Cupid, draw back thy bow & let thy arrow go straight to my lover's
Heart for me! We are cooking up a storm. A tornado that drips
Down the side. For protection we run into a yellow tent.

Greece

To sleep in—tick-tock. I can't set the alarm for your next
        emergency,
It will emerge in a gong of blush some hot o'clock when Love

is finally

Unrationed and joins her cousin, Irrational. We must go and pull
out the poison

Ivy, friend, hand by hand. Then we will walk across fire, save
the icon in the pine

Forest, pluck hot ouzo bottle from charred bucket, and douse our
sponge (head)

In song. The simple life, sky as hat. Earning our daily bread
by swimming the old

Mill stream, stirring up water so the big wheel keeps on turning
as the grist

Grinds itself. The doctor nods patiently, wearily, expectantly,
nervously, and

Delivers an "Is that so?" so delicately that you know it is just so,
that you hadn't

Realized just how so it was. That old so-and-so, he was just so-so.
Sheesh, if

I were you, I'd resign effective immediately and get a day job
of some sort, a

Carhop, or a surveyor. Part II. It is very important to forget an
occasional meal,

To allow that officious Team of Socializers to betray themselves.
Ach! The wine-

Dark sea was never winier, he cracked, but I heard "whinier" as the
Aegean begged

To list its complaints. A typo? On and on it went, a curvy trail up
Mt. Olympus.

What happened was they needed the top! Part III. In the blink of a
wink she had

Wrapped me in a sheet, but I did not know if I were a shrouded
corpse, a toga-ed

God, or a sauna-toweled tool. I was completely in her hands, beautifully calloused,

Exquisitely veined. In the Land of Statues, they sculpted the living, and she was

The Ideal. Such subtlety in the mouth, an abstract kiss, possessing a spirit so

Generous—I was stopped altogether. No recourse. The language couldn't contain

Us, hopelessly sentiment-filled as it was. Iron filings burst into bloom. As for

You who want more words: Keep still. Observe. And memorize "Forms in the Sky."

Orgy in Unusual Company

A poor man looking forward to a pleasant night
    Slick hair and libidinous glance
Only a revolution could make him successful
    Knee-deep in scruples
            Here's his chance!
        Not yet in love, but falling

Last Year's Tight

If ever you forget this scene
You would be the most despicable of all:
A curable romantic!
Progress is so damn noisy,
Here where life begins.

Goo Ahead

Goo ahead

The Collect Call of the Wild

Here it is, just where you said
It would be. Your mind is quiet
& your shoes, well, they seem to be going
Somewhere. The road, the road, as was once
Said, or twice, is where we go on. Where

Everything is acceptable, the blame more
Than most. Gray hair, cigarettes, tightening
Pants. To be gored by age is not exactly sexy,
But it's not to be denied. Not anymore.
Not any less, either, as the sun earnestly plies

The window dressing. A vocabulary, not the secret
Of life, that's all. If it taxes your spirit,
Some kind of government must be flowering. Blood
Is one example, the example of constancy, readiness
& effulgence. Another is lit up like Reno, popped

Champagne & caviar on a paper plate. What does
Doesn't last, & what is lost will probably
Transform even if it's found. That's the problem,
That the idea of the thing won't stand still,
A doggie finding its spot. Which name *is* Spot.

Of course the pay phone rings in the crowded lunch,
With no one caring the slightest for its emergency.
Too many crackers in the soup, the glass is greasy,
Yet we rest easy. It's the company, I'd guess.
That we finally have accepted knowing each other this way,
& that's the way we find ourselves, little by little, by & large.

3

BEACH SIMPLIFIES HORIZON

Here warmly framed in gold, the young Cézanne
Would scratch his pen neath the solemn eyes of Zola
And run his letters together cryptomorphically
So that the Rhône would hush and ever so
Sweetly the Rhône would hush as in Zola's eye
A single tear would work its way out and down,
In the center of town, the muffled drum
And a clear blue memory of a man whose pipe
Would not draw but work a puff of smoke
About and around like friendship

I would, that longest window, sit there
And grapple with morning. With the chair
Appropriately turned on its side, narrow,
Opalescent, triangulated, waiting night's
Fountain and lots of music everywhere

Sometimes I smoke
Sometimes my pants fall down
But it's ok
I wear underpants
I don't smoke in bed

This, woman, is bread
We eat the stuff
That's how it happens

Not a care in the garden
So I'll stay there, grappling
With no care, caressing the tender
Hair of your whiteness, where color
Once was, and pouring water, and I am red

Touch a moment
That, baby, is so good
And my huge forearm
Big gulps and gulps
And also to turn around
And see you there

Green did someone say
Green lots of green
All over the place you'll find green
That's what I mean
Simply green

Once there was light
We'd sit in it
Maybe a wall
Isn't a bright idea

Let's take a fat shower together
And mix up our hairs
And kiss whatever
And a blind lover
Just make it sweet

Escape from land
Jump in and disappear

This is the life
So cool and long

100 years of a rose
And my beach simplifies the horizon
Please get dressed in a relaxed manner
While I watch and watch

The sun of melody
I mean the sun's melody
Humming wind
All right, I'll lift my arm

Solid and airy, and clumsy Beauty
Put an arm up if you are
Well whatever you are doing you
Can always put your arm up
Or maybe just put your arm up
Maybe with a lot of blue water
You'll lift something and it will be
You, your arm and you, blue too

We'll invite over just scads of people
If it's ok with you and eat fruit,
        all different kinds
Maybe you'll take your clothes off
Maybe Paul will draw you with
        that magic brush of his
We could probably stay like that
        probably forever

The only thing
You can wear

Is your tattoo

What are you thinking about
I am thinking about screaming
That makes me laugh and your smile
And life's relay scream a song

It sounds funny
To get in bed
Like hand me a knife
I'll cut a hole
In the puffy mattress
And we can crawl in there

Beds, please don't
Sleep on them
They are our friends

This tree is now the sun
And all the bathers are wearing
Glasses. Well, are they
        sunglasses?
Ask for yourself. They
Will answer, and that will
Be it for you you

This is not paradise, it is
Marvelous, about 5 km outside
Paradise. I was born and raised
In this tent and yesterday it fell
Down. I don't care. Let it rain.
I'll eat your hair without a

Care and press my trousers but
Where did I leave my trousers?

Paul, hurry! The Bathers are dancing
They're balling the hillside and a
Barking shadow warns them if you're
Not careful. They are practicing
Safe sex and look like they'll graduate
With honors. That's the story, but
Where is the painting? Paul, come back,
You have forgotten the easel, the paints,
The pants, the. . . .

Time to join in with time
All the time is just a mouth
The corpse leaps out of the coffin
As the bone from your forehead
It means fight, and we will,
With swords and shields and
Sleeping you fight me back awake

What's wrong with this picture
Nothing
That is what is wrong
And a beer glass

I'll just sit down here and rest
While you do the rest

For goodness sake
Don't you think
You've carried that water jug

Far enough
To the moon and back
And to the moon

Colors are something else
For example, a fence
That softens a little

I think I've found a niche
In this rock
Or maybe my buttocks
Made it
But I'll stay here
To consider

Which way
This way
Or that way
Always

All there is
In the big room
Is the walls of
The room
And paintings paintings

That says it
That says it all
Except no fair
Saying it

A jungle of white towels
On brightest July mid-morning

I'm running into irony
But you keep pulling me back
Little by little

Caught in the polka of the soul
I was a brat with a mission
Listen to me, for I'll say it but once
And now, having forgot what it was,
Come back, genuine idea of it,
I cannot run anymore

Maybe it's time we got wet
Only our reflections
The rest is sex and sun
And somebody explaining it to you
        with a tongue

Hey you
Yeah
You look great
You too
Totally great in front of me

What were we saying
I forget but maybe
We can conjure up a telephone
Then the telephone would remember
That is what they are for

Who moved that bridge to there
No, they built it
And it was always there
Go back to sleep

What are we doing now
What were we ever doing
We are being flowers, tulips
And we are looking at you
With that "join us" look as
We join too, everything, that
Is what we are doing, or
Did, joining up and in and becoming
Everything, everything is what we are

I'm not sure, or,
No longer am I sure
But yes it seems
It seems a boat
So after that
After that I don't

Maybe the sun
Again, maybe not
Or who is over there
I'm surprised it's you
You used to but it's ok
You did, I remember the
Time, but then time joined up
Sweet and swift, this silence

4

PANIC * DJ!

Hey, What'd I Say?

I talk this way but I don't stop
The way this does
Sometimes

Language arches direct

These words held so tight

Which is another characteristic
This stepping in & out of different uh
Characteristics & characters
Not real characters though . . .
(Lordy, he does go on!) Could someone else . . .

The words themselves!
Little trills,
Slippery darlings,
So full of meaning
That I forget to say
The grace of words as they
are written, the action
of words as they are spoken, & the trust
of the air that carries them—O air! Carry them
to ears that hear!

We'd be kissing

But I'm too busy talking

Without saying it in some kind of carry persona
Like "Tends to go on"
Not that I would ever use a phrase
That it tends to go on
There is that element of my speech

SWEAT&SEX&POLITICS!

Sweat & sex & politics.
Sweat & sex & politics?
Sweat & sex & politics!
That's the way I get my kicks!

Thought is made in the mouth
You don't think of it—until you rap it out
You gotta raprap till everything gets said
You gotta raprap—are you living in yr head?
Pondering, wandering
Floundering aroundering
Communicate! Reciprocate!
Conversate! Don't hesitate.
In the beginning . . . was the Rap!

Get the beat with the beat
That's the beat beat beat
Quietude, solitude
Gratitude to multitude
Yr mama's calling up to you
She wants do—what'd she say to do?—
Rap it up!

But then the phone rings, you get to start up again
Say excuse me, apologize to yr friends
Use the receiver, a new conversation begins
Pass the phone around, integrate all yr friends
Live disco-ussions! Get 'em on tape
Blow up thought balloons, words just gotta escape
Try the HELP! rap when yr in a tight scrape
When you get the chance don't bite your tongue just let it dance

Harmonize, soliloquize
Rhapsodize, ventriloquize
Even little baby cries . . . are raps!

Cause rapping is just writing when the writing's on the wall
But the wall is gone. There ain't no wall at all.
Words fall, words full
Wonderful! A waterfall!
Round the rap and have a ball
& on & on & on on y on
& on & **on** & ON!

Sweat & sex & politics!
That's the way I get my kicks!
On a toot with the Absolute
If you want to know the truth . . .

There's a feeling across the nation
Is this season's be-true-to sensation
When you realize it's a pack of lies
Been dealt from the bottom then there's no surprise
You can pick it up, you can put it down
You can sell it from a pushcart all over town
You can paint it on the walls of the Lost & Found
How can you see the light when you're living underground?

O show me the way to the next sushi bar!

Kick the door in! Kick the floor in!
Fallout shelters are so boring!
Loud Fast Rules cool in our high schools
Nuke your teach whilst on the beach
Just take a page from *The Book of Rage*
Microchip-chip-chippin' your life away . . .

Hey, you! Makin' it new? Doncha know that that'll do?
There's only now, any how, which, way that you cut it
If and or but it just goes on & on & on doncha know
On & on . . . Say, excuse me. Say, sorry to interrupt—
But there's something that I just gotta discuss
It's the word *Word* with the language on the side
It's the *Rap* rap with your ears as a guide!
Wordslide! Tide's right.
Rap the rap all through the night.
1 2 3 4 Who you gonna shshshsh for?

Say yr sleeping but say yr lover's awake
And yr dreaming, when the earth starts to quake
And you hear screaming as yr given a shake . . .
You were rapping in yr sleep!
Those dream secrets just won't keep
Raps are dreams that spring a leak
We're talking Dream Rap, we're talking D r e a m R a p . . .

Like the butcher with the meat
Ties the packages so neat
He's a raprapraprap rapper
Like olympic athlete
With olympic athlete's feet
She's a raprapraprap rapper
Rap it up! Spit it out!
From a whisper to a shout. . . .
Why don't you rap to me now in that voice which even now in
Anticipation of it has
Reduced me to a Sub-modern Post-Semiomortician!
Ooooooooooooooooo!

―――――

Rapping away, crazy all the way
Rapping to yourself? Have you rapped yours today?
The more you have to say, the more you have to say it
And the more you have to say it—the more you have to say!
You have to rap! You have to rap?
You have the right to rap!
You have to write to rap?
Oooooooooooooooooo!

Stop my rapping? Stop my breathing you mean!
You see, a rapper is not a rapping machine
Once you turn me on, don't say, "Turn off!" I mean,
Don't say "Shut your trap!" to the Freedom of the Rap!
Where the rap's at's where it's at
When you're a raprap rapraprap raprapraprapraprapraprap Rapper!

Take off that cryptic lipstick
And make-up your mi-yi-yi-yi-yind!

So I leave you
With one little rap
Don't you rap it!
Unless you want to rap back
Don't you bag it
Once the words begin to flow
It's to and fro with those bon mots
Let's rap it up to go
Let's rap it up, let's rap it up
Rapidrapidrapid, wrapitwrapitwrapit
Rap it rap it rap it
Rap it up!

Up!

Beside Myself if not delighted

      having learned how the damn typewriter works
        and forgiven myself all the daily errors I so
          readily and compulsively commit & recommit:

I dedicate myself to the utter continuation, to the ongoingness
    of possibility, volunteering blood itself into the lifestreams
      of beings as different as the individual letters that make up
        the words that try to say what they mean.

Intuitive pulses race and won't settle; these tracings
    being designed as a whetter, whistler, and whatchamacallit . . .
      You can put me down, but you can't put it down—
        what's done is done. I take it back.

In the golden horizon replete with all language, I dreamed
    I was in past & you were there, this is getting closer.
      The excitement of I got you covered & knowledge
        springing truth free as trout over water, hallelujah!

Meanwhile the bastards have occupied where we go back to.
    There is nothing, so blindly we keep digging for the ground
      under the ground and around the hole, ah
        until looking for something is finding it.

It's all that's left. That is what you are thinking.
    This is the first time I've been able to read your thoughts.
      I'm surprised at how enclosed you are. Like a fence
        that never corners, traveling ever forever

& never touching. We are not the only exceptions.
    We are simply exceptional. The driver, the driven—
        here in the sun we can shrug, pretend to laugh it off
        all the while knowing we'll never know

And in the end we can ask how we got here. Looking around
    over this is all ours, breath itself enough to die from.
        The lyric came from the heart, you respond, quoting my
        thought back to me. You will always. & I will too.

Cowboy Heaven

    I usta eat my share of dogfood
    Usta chaw on the old milky bone
    Usta keep myself in stitches
    Every time I answered the phone

    There ain't a single bar stool I ain't sat at
    Walk in circles, say, I get around
    Adjust my ears & the air & the juke-box
    Till Willie Nelson sounds like he's on downs

    & the phone's a-ringing in my room
    Can't find the key in the light of the moon
    I'm sure it's COWBOY HEAVEN that's calling
    & I'll have to answer real soon

    Last night I finished *The Power of Positive Drinking*
    Got drunk stayed drunk moaned drunk bleat drunk blubbery drunk
        wept drunk punchy drunk puke drunk mean drunk wild drunk
        wicked drunk wacky drunk falling down getting back up drunk

falling down staying down drunk drunk as sin punk drunk skunk
drunk
& if my system survives it
I'll get it out of my system

& the phone keeps a-ringing! & that's my room
& I can't find the key, maybe I left it in my other pants, but where
did I leave my other pants? Maybe I dropped the key on the floor
here . . . Does anybody have one of those pocket disposable flash-
lights? Cause I'm sure that it's COWBOY (not COWGIRL!
nor COWMAN!! surely not COWWOMAN!!! but
COWBOY) HEAVEN!!!! that's calling
& I'll have to answer real soon

Cellular Phone

Tiffany night light
Dior sheets
Wind up my Piaget clocks
Gravlax appy
Godiva sweets
Lay out my Perry Ellis socks

Tiny refrigerator
By my bed
Close the door, the light stays on
Would you like a blue Margarita?
Frozen Heinie instead?
I could micro up some instant swan

I'm never at home
   I'm never alone

I'm on the cellular phone
With you

Can't sleep a wink
My Cuisinart's on the blink
Time for a Home Shopping Network shopping spree
Pesto pizza with caviar
Delivered to my Internet boudoir
Tune into my divorce on Court TV

Can't get no satisfaction
From my Range Rover's 4-wheel traction
How'm I gonna tramp round the country house?
Redo the Jag
Some nice paisley shag
Can't forget smoked aspic for the grouse

I'm never at home
  I'm never alone
    I'm on the cellular phone
With you

Next week at St. Bart's
We'll be intertransplanting our hearts
Take a peek at a designer satellite dish
The art of Kostabi
So much more than a hobby
This wholehearted sprouted Danish is delish

Oola & toute suite
Bring on the mesquite
Plank the Chinook on the Weber barbecue
Please don't sit on

The Dom Perignon
Does Spiro Agnew really live next door to you?

I'm never at home
   I'm never alone
      I'm on the cellular phone
With you

There's nothing to fear
   Making love ear-to-ear
      Making cellular love
With you

Zooin' in Alphabet Town

for David Henderson

Blank spaces
Between buildings
Hadn't been there

Ooo, a little squirming
In a zoo now
Be cool
In the center
Don't get picked off
At the end
Of the line
To be eaten

Piles of rubbish
Broken glass & cans & jewels
Shimmering rubbish
Artificial moon

Neon blink
Between A & B
CLUB round & round
Neon blink
Good times here
Put together by one or two people
It's not like they're part
Of an international chain
Except the international chain of
No cover   No minimum
No maximum   To the good times

Sign says Free Public Baths
Sign says Wholesale Vegetable Distributor

Big tapestry, brilliant
Jesus. *Jésus!* Window
Slams down.

Sidewalk covered with acronyms
HEW, HUD. Asbestos.
The man who invented asbestos
Died a few years later
Of lung cancer
All the builders insulated with it
Madison Square insulated with it
Until the elephants knocked it down

Nuyorican girls club
Teen Angels go
For a young boy's legs
Sweet torment, 6th St.

Well, the liquor store on Avenue C
Now there's a sight
Hard to get a bottle
Even when you got the money
Security door, bullet-proof plexiglass
Attack-train doberman shepherd
Hey, that liquor sure is priceless stuff

Roaming around food aromas
Bread baking
Ripe mangoes for a second
Did you get that
For a second strong mango
Tropical moon music

Music music music

7th between B & C
Right before dawn
Pushcart people
In the distance
Comin' up
Comin' up
Avenue C
From down below Houston St.
Settle down
Light little fires
Like a Gypsy caravan
It really was
Fruits, vegetables, candles
Mangoes? Not then

Not for long
With the Lower East Side Charcuterie
Do you accept food stamps for your paté?
mythCappuccino would be fine
Chevre & a nice lite wine

Hey, look over there
What used to be a Camaro
Parked where a building used to be
All the glass broken out
All the windows in the building broken out
It's in the right place
No tires
Not going anywhere
It takes a lot of cinder blocks
To seal up
The city cracks

Put that Camaro in a museum!

Crossing Avenue A
Feeling the DMZ
On 11th St., Paradise Alley
Kerouac wrote here
Then a shooting gallery
Now the junkies are blocked in

At one time neigh' highly Jewish
Yeshiva here
The Irish controlling the waterfront
So the Jewish kids didn't go swimming

On 3rd St. some row houses
Hamilton Fish built them
Middle class, 1830's
7th St. bourgeoisie

Yo! Peace Eye Books
Kosher Dairy
Allen Ginsberg ate here
Muggers left his poems
Poems still here

Graffiti
I remember

What it said
I don't remember

Beauty image
Street-lit

Images sustain community
Gentrification cuts out
Music music music

The garbage
Hell I wrote a letter
Three days later
Two garbagemen
Came to the door

OK OK, let's trace it
Inside the detail
Let's trace the origins of garbage

Remember Lionel Ziffrin,
Famous (Zif) comics founder
Wandering late at night
Collecting icons
Old Ukrainian ones, homemade ones
Agents of Christianity also out late at night
Out to destroy the icons
Battle of the Icons

Several places, they built their own icons
Birds on sheets, crate altars
Jars of liquid amphetamine
With different colored pebbles in them
People working all the time all the time
& then somebody flipping out
& trashing the whole place

Stomping in the night! Amphetaminos!

Reality sense community
Pockets of beauty
Survival music
Get it together before it disappears

The people the buildings & whatnot
People out there, life
Goes on in its everyday
Disaster area

Up on 75th & 5th with a beer on the street
Illegal to drink there, babes
Except Perrier
In a paper bag

Down here *Esquire* photoed some bums
Then polished them
Before & After
Now they're rich Hollywood stars
With agents
Now they're back on the Bowery
Wined

A bag lady listening through the door salsas

Tripping on D at 2 or 3
Sinister street
But keep it looking messed up
Maybe the gentry can't set up shop

In the apartments it's cozy
Outside, the garbage is camouflage
When the streets get cleaned up
The people who've been living here
Won't be able to afford to anymore

Painted walls
Empty buildings
Darkness at twilight

Recipe

It was late
& I had sat down under a tree to rest
The breeze started up, very lightly
Cool on my skin, the hairs on my arm quivered
I was in the middle years of my life
& the sun was running a race with me

I was full of dreams, unrealized selves
& felt melancholic, of an even despair
I wrote myself a note
Actually, it was a recipe
For a pudding
I would never make
Nor taste
It was so 14th Century
It was a jewel, the pen flew
An enigma: how much sugar if any
& suddenly the present was everywhere
Youthful, florid, & apprised
I was a tourist, & the tree was my border guard
Soon the hated birds would be pecking the earth again
I would make the pudding!
I would make the pudding!

Where Do You Get Off?

Past the suburbs of languor, your vagina
Laughs and my penis introduces self. There
Are many beds, I am told, but there's only one
With you in it, and here I am in it with you.
One raindrop from a dizzying height, that's what
Is falling straight for the boing of a daffodil
Blossom's kiss. Yumbo. Smack. Around you
There always seems space for me, my shadow
Precedes me, eases the way, cuts a form
I fill up exactly. Maybe go too far, say it
And it is, not like this is at all. Finding
Myself staring at me through your eyes, I think
Only I never think at all, how did this happen?

THE IMPOSSIBLE RAP

Last night as I was passing into sleep
One final thought began to race me to the dream
Intercepting the sweet powers of Morpheus
Pressing me to wakefulness and purpose

I drew my pen and prepared to set down this marvel,
Final thought of my existence—so it seemed—
The thought itself panting, near Death, as I
Retrieved it: it called itself, The Other Thought

What? A thought appearing in my mind that's not of my
Thinking? A thought I thought I'd exiled that thought,
Banished it as not of me, not **me** enough, then urging
Me to *Please shut up,* The Other Thought continued:

"Do not dwell upon the political implications inherent in your
Inability to entertain any but your own precious thoughts, Buddy.
Rather, amend your ways to allow The Other Thought's existence.
Write not The Poem; write The Other Poem!" 'Tis impossible!

I countered, for by so doing, by giving vent to The Other,
Am I not precluding the very basis of my own existence, essence
Of *me?* At that, the thought became a shiver that coursed
My spine, and I find myself engaged in application:

To rap the rap with the truest groove
There's no stop-gap from the first remove
This either/or thing
Is just one more thing
A touch too much
A tad too bad
A bit to wit

A might too tight
Explode in your mind, a tiny grenade
Leaving the impression The Other Thought made
I never thought . . .
I never thought The Other Thought

Hey, wait a second
Wait a second second
This is Impossible!

The Impossible Rap
Is ready to appear
Is it possible that
You are ready to hear
It has something to do
With what you just said
It's the thought you can't remember
In the back of your head
It's the dream you won't surrender
When you get out of bed
Just Return to Sender
Think The Other Thought instead
The Other Thought's gonna get you

If you say rapping is just scratching on the surface
I think I know what's making you so nervous
You say you don't understand the beat?
Put your ears to the ground and listen to your feet

It's Impossible!
But undeniable
It's ubiquitous
Don't hold me liable

It's always behind you
When you turn around
Just out of sight
Just underground

Might as well go to bed
Chill that hot-thought head
Good night! Sleep tight.
Twixt waking & sleeping
The Other Thought is seeping
Creeping & leaping into place
Right before your face
With a certain grace
Well, in that case:
Is it Impossible
Sine qua known
It's a itsy-bitsy schizy
Other Thought's on the phone
It's so humiliating when your brain is on call waiting
It's so humiliating when your brain is on call waiting

Back back back
Back before you said it
Back back back
Back before you thought
You were there too
How do you do?
Is your thinking on the blink
What is it to you
Can't tell what from . . . what-not?
It's what The Other Thought's Thought thought

That's real clear
You can take your tongue out of my ear
Another Other Thought is surfacing
While the surface disappears

Caramba! (Take a number)
Caramba! (Take a number)
Get in line with your mind
Get in line with your mind

I'm in with the Out Crowd
The Other Thought's cryin' out loud

Take the alternate take the alternate take the alternate take . . .

The rush to resolution is not a solution

The Impossible Rap
Is ready to appear
Is it possible that
You are ready to hear
It has something to do
With what you just said
It's the thought you can't remember
In the back of your head
It's the dream you won't surrender
When you get out of bed
Just Return to Sender
Think The Other Thought instead

TRANSCEND
THE END

Perfect

Everything's so right
Flower right where it should be
Birds singing all in tune
The spring wind is full of feeling
Blowing my silk dress open

Harmony

Every time I stand up I drift away
At every occurrence I am astonished
That is the sun making the river run
All of a sudden, it's an old tune
The rain watering the flower in my lapel

Love

for Elizabeth

Your hand throws out
As you sleep

And brushes
Another body

Lands and settles
On the other body

Except it is your hand
And it is my body

The Proposal

It was a brisk morning as I watered the garden,
hose in one hand, cigarette in the other,
the grass tickling as it grew against my feet.
My vision was 20/20 and all I could see were
images of myself mirrored in the bougainvillea
and ornamental fruit trees. The fog was sweeping
easterly, and I reflected on these images which were
themselves reflections until I had reduced all thought
to one thought, all images to one image.

An electric surge coursed through my body, followed
by the slight rustling sound of light breeze through willow,
which in turn signalled a total silence
accompanied by a faint hint of ozone,
as if a great storm were brewing, a storm, I realized with a start,
that was centered inside myself! I felt a strange, prickly sensation,
like fright climbing the spine, in my lungs and heart, and suddenly
I was struck by the understanding
that what I was feeling was my own inner Self
loosening from me like a wad of phlegm and freeing along with it
all the Angels and Demons which I now saw frozen in postures
of frightful opposition inside me. Immediately, this crowd physicalized
on the tip of my nose and began cavorting merrily, dissolving and
reforming from a field of motes, while my Self,
in the form of a gray cloud, slipped
through my nose as an exhalation, encompassing the Dancers.
This cloud cast off then, sailing gently into the fog, which in turn
was encompassed by a greater fog, a grayness which came
from behind me and covered everything,
completely filling my field of vision,
as I slipped into this grayness myself an exhalation.

I awoke, fog gone, sun brilliant overhead, the garden all around me.
It was a glorious day—birds, insects, tiny frogs all in concert,
and I lifted the cigarette to my lips, but it had gone out, leaving
only the filter, which I tossed down, noticing that the grass had grown
up between my toes. The hose had slowed to a trickle, and I pulled
my penis out and arched a gold stream, showering the earth.
Thus relieved, I turned
back to the house, where I could hear the stirrings of
She
whom I now knew I would marry.

Night

Night put on its enormous hat
& started imitating me behind my back
I whirled around so quickly
I walked right out of there & kept walking

Night set out after me, calling
But I was so cool
I just kept on walking & walking
To this very day walking

Required Reading

The air
Grew so heavy
All our imagination
Was required
To free the birds
From the clouds

Malvinas

Archbishop Falderol is on a mission
To ease the dying to death
A pot of geraniums to rest their luverly heads . . .
Slogging through the porridge from Goose Green to Darwin
On the great battlefields of Los Falklands
Exocets burst through the waves of el blammo
(Can you read me? No, I never learned to read)

All they had me doing was hopping these little Harrier jets
Like a toad on a ball field (squish squish)
Sloshing through the fields of bloody penguins . . .
O, Lost Islands, who would think such an accident
As your lonely coordinates could be so directly in the line of fire?
(No damn radar but evil killer lust suffices rrr)

I'm ashamed of my weapons (& those who built them)
Admiral Poobah in his funny hat (yi-yi)
We peed from on top of the hen house
Onto the campfires of our enemy

People who lived to be buried in land blowtorched for graveholes
Bury them not in bomb craters
Build missile sites on these foundations
Brine, kelp, blood, crap
1800 people lived here, more than that now dead, fighting for
Spitball of land, meatlocker, humanity's deep freeze . . . Malvinas!

The Meaning of Meaning

I don't have any idea
Would you like to play a game of Clue

Is there anything you've said you'd like to talk about
Is there anything you wouldn't do

> I've put my foot down so many times it feels like
> I'm walking. Stick foot in mouth just to get rolling!
> Got head screwed on tight all right. Frantically
> sleeping! My teeth have lost their bite . . .

What's the meaning of Meaning
What's the purpose of Purpose
What's the use—can I use it?
It feels so good to refuse it

O, I get it—the answer's not related to the question
It illuminates a completely different plane
But then the plane takes a loopity-loop nosedive to the runaway
But don't worry—the song always goes for the refrain

> I'm talking about the progressing progressions of a song
> into its resultant resolving resolution—Talking 'bout
> a Resolution, o Yeah . . . Shake it up Baby, Shake & Twist . . .
> Wouh-woah

What's the meaning of Meaning
What's the purpose of Purpose
What's the use—can I use it?
It feels so good to refuse it

Ooo, don't you cry on my metaphysical Hit Parade
(Scared the joke right out of its wits today!)
I mean to say, in terms of saying
It hurts to have a metaphysical hit

> OK. I'd like to propose that nothing's on purpose, the purpose
> of which is to assure you that there's no meaning to Meaning

in the first place—But, in the second place, you understand,
a very fine line separating the one hand "To mean" but on the
other hand I mean . . .

What's the meaning of Meaning
What's the purpose of Purpose
What's the use—can I use it?
It feels so good to refuse it

Usher

This is the true story of an Usher who gets called to the stage when
the star gets sick. It all happens so fast she has to do the part while
still dressed in her usher's uniform. But unbelievably, her perfor-
mance is so great, so believable, that everyone in the audience swears
they saw her wearing the star's red nightgown. In fact, so many peo-
ple mention this that other people get suspicious, and finally the en-
tire audience is ordered to undergo lie detector tests.

The audience members report to individual rooms for their poly-
graphs, while the friends and relatives who accompanied them wait in
a huge antechamber. Here, after an initial tense silence, pleasant con-
versations are struck up. Through the idlest of chatter, certain simi-
larities of habit of the audience members are noted, strange
coincidences and patterns.

By the time the polygraphs are over, many discoveries have been
made. When the audience members leave their tiny cubicles, those
waiting for them clam up immediately. The audience members are
sweaty, shaken, furtive; it is clear that many of them flunked the
tests. Gradually, a giant conspiracy is uncovered, a conspiracy led by
the Usher, who has developed a whole new theory of the theatre.

Red-Tailed Hawk Feather

Today I found a Red-tailed Hawk feather
And I wondered what it meant.
I figured it to be an omen,
Holding it in the light.
I thought I'd write a poem about it.
That's what it means,
I get a poem out of it!
So you can read it
And tell me what it means.
It means there is one bare-assed hawk!
No, I'm sure the hawk barely misses it.
But—*why me, Lord?*
Why should I be the one to whom this should befall, hmm?
Lucky thing a poet found this feather.
It's enough to drive me bananas!

Awake in the belly of night,
With digestion all around,
I pull out the feather and pursue my analysis—
Waiting for the individual featherettes to fall out
And leave me alone with the feather bone, or "quill,"
With which I write to convey the feather.

And now, O dear and patient Reader, you have heard the tale.
It is nearing another tedious sunrise on this planet of worms.
Take this insidious task from me!
Here, take the feather,
And go after worms!

Pasta Mon

Pasta Mon cookin' in a limousine
Windows rolled up—poem written' in the steam
Poem starts to change—to a recipe?
I'm cookin' up a story! You still hungry?

Deep in the blue sea deep in the memory
Connected, perfected—totally poetry
Yuppie got a puppy & the baby got a pamper
Doin' the 500 in a Winnebago camper

Why?
Why?
Why Pasta Mon cry?

Back in the history I shot the deputy
For not makin' sauce sufficiently garlicky
Everyone connected in a single ecstasy
We're a single strand of Pasta Mon's linguini

This is the wild life! Carbohydrates, out of sight
Pasta Mon Fashions give eyesight insight
See the world through spaghetti headlights
Wear a ravioli figleaf! It's a Pasta Paradise!

Why?
Why?
Fresh onions is why

So much pasta Mon cannot give it away
What's the matter with a platter of pasta paté?
Keep the homefries burnin'—a sorbet gourmet?
You too can have your own authentic Pasta Mon beret

Pasta Mon starrin' on his own tv show
Yesterday's menu's already obsolete-o
Shows you how to roll a pasta-filled burrito
We'll be right back after this break with Pasta Mon Vito

BREAK

(Bob) What's for dindin?
(Vito) Pasta.
          Mon.
Pass the Pasta Pan.

It might boil over—the pot is bubblin'
It might boil over it's your mind that's troublin'
It might boil over—dynamite
Might boil away to nuttin', spoil your appetite

It happened to me while reading Weekly Reader
The future was coming—it would be beater
Beater, deffer, bigger forever
Sun on the horizon—it's always risin'

What's happenin'?
(I'm just askin')
What happened?
Huh?

The Future is here—the Past is a goner
All baked in a pasta shell of once upon a
Time when the rhyme was flora and fauna
Cheese syntheses: Utopian lasagna

A nickel for a can & a nickel for a bottle
A trickle down sound from the nickel that bought ya
America the Beautiful in quarantine
A cardboard mattress & a cardboard dream

What's happenin'?
(I'm just askin')
What happened?
Huh?

Barbecue trashcans linin' the Hudson
The dogs are howlin' as you throw the spuds on
Pasta Mon's recipes gettin' verra smelly
Rat ratatouille & vermin vermicelli

It might boil over the pot is bubblin'
It might boil over it's your mind that's troublin'
It might boil over—dynamite
Might boil away to nothin', spoil your appetite

What's happenin'?
(I'm just askin')
What happened?
Huh?

YOU CAN'T BE A JERK & WRITE GREAT POETRY

you can't be a jerk & write great poetry
no you can't be an asshole & plumb the depths of the spirit
you can be clever, you can be accurate as to form
but it's simply yr jumbo ego on the line, that's right

yr vision will ever be clouded uh huh
& yr ideas will always need sharpening
like a kid at the pencil sharpener
whose point keeps breaking over & over
as the kid grinds away & the pencil
just keeps getting shorter & shorter . . .

so wake up, you turkey romantics
& stop treating everyone like shit
yeah, you can't be a jerk & write great poems, lissen to me now
you can't treat other people like shit & not pay for it in yr art, it's
     true

I mean, what do you think, the world's at yr service,
existing solely in yr brain,
waiting adoringly for you to etch a line or two in some porcelain
while meanwhile yr friends & lovers run away at yr hideous
     approach?

wise up, señor y señora saps!
before I start spilling the delicious venom

I relish the thought of yr beatific (ha) eyes
searching the corners of yr mess, searching
for a thought, any thought, something
to fill the hole of yr deserted imagination

help! I'm being held prisoner by everything I say!
breath itself enough to die from!
I was born an only alphabet!

It was all a pipe dream where you smoke the pipe itself & not the
tobacco, or, as some smart Belgian once said, having smoked his

pipe, & painted a picture of it from memory, this is not a pipe.
only he wrote it in French, so no one would ever know.

there's something to be said for it
but you don't know what it is
there's something that's the point of it
but yv got it all wrong
yr standing on the verge of it
but yv forgot which direction yr going
you don't even trip over yr own feet anymore
yr so busy bouncing on yr head

the director shouts, "Rolling!"
& you tumble right in front of the camera

understand, yr impulse was right
it was just too fast

you can't be a jerk & write great poetry

STRONG CURTAIN

I'd Rather Be Crazy Than Stupid

(SO HOW COME I'M CRAZY FOR YOU?)

If you're crazy, you're crazy—you've just gone round the bend
When you're stupid you just keep on bendin' in the wind
Loving you is as dumb now as when this thing just begin
I may be crazy for you now—but I'm just stupid in the end

[spoken] Second Verse

It was a dream. Why do we dream? What's the purpose of a dream?

I got a job. I know my job. I'm good at it, it seems.
I live alone. Well, there's the dog. But he don't really count.
Then there's you—you got the trailer, and your husband, he's a
    friend.

[spoken] It gets worse . . .

I wish the men in the white coats'd come take me off
A dark padded cell's better'n this living hell
O please—won't you leave me! Love me! or grieve for me!
Call up the hospital! Do it now!

[spoken] 911

My face in the mirror looks like a weed.
Not the tall well-kept sapling I was once't.
Time goes by. That's my cry. Not a coyote in the county.
They're after me! *I got no brain!* I'M GOING CRAZY!

[spoken] God I wish

If you're crazy, you're crazy—you've just gone round the bend
When you're stupid you just keep on bendin' in the wind
Loving you is as dumb now as when this thing just begin
I may be crazy for you now, but I'm just stupid in the end

Only One Love Song

You know, sometimes it gets mighty lonely
Sitting here writing poems to change the world
That's why I'm so glad I've got you to be with
& my thoughts slip from this mess that keeps me awake
    to you sleeping . . .

66

———

Why can't I come right out & say it
What's the matter with me now
Why can't I just tell the truth
What's stopping me anyhow

I look around & I can't see you
I know you didn't go away
I just had my eyes closed, didn't I
Trying to think of words to say—

I just want to write one love song
Only one. Only one. You are my only one . . .
I want to write only one love song
& it's you

There's got to be some way to get this together
The personal, political, art
What's all this talk add up to, anyway
What if I just sing it from the heart

It's not that I don't love you
It's not that love has changed
It's just the way things been going lately
Maybe that's why I'm saying

I just want to write one love song
Only one. Only one. You are my only one . . .
I want to write only one love song
& it's you

We read the books, the papers
We talk politics, we talk feelings, we keep at it

& that's why I have such trouble with the pop notion of "Love Song"!
They don't feel like real love at all, & make me angry,
& I pound around on the typewriter, & now I realize that I woke
   you up—
Here, a love song! For you! See,

I just want to write one love song
Only one. Only one. You are my only one . . .
I want to write only one love song
& it's you

ROCK'N'ROLL MYTHOLOGY

gotta ROCK'N'ROLL MYTHOLOGY
gotta Total Apocalypse Pathology
got the most PostHysterical Poetry
& if it ain't comin' at you then it's breezed on by

got the heavy-duty political intent
got the worm farm free-form diamond noodle content
I got breezy ways & boppin' rays
when the word explodes the mother lode is where I'm at

& it's light here but you cannot see
doesn't matter anyway since you cannot breathe
you see the words mean, they're putting on the squeeze
that could strangle you—hey, what's that mean

say what he say
say what he say
he said he say
he said he said

say what he said
go on & say he said
what'd he say he said
that's what he said
that's what he said to say
he said to say

open up the book w/ yr finger hook
& scan it w/ yr television eyes
(televisionize televisionize televisionize televisionize)
fuck it w/ yr eyes
stick out yr tongue & memorize
it's just you reading
the book is breathing
time's new dimension settles in

you are dancing on the edge of a thin thin dime
cause you are marching to the phone booth w/ a refugee line
you are baking in the kitchen when the walls cave
you are crawling through the desert w/ a loony rave
you are crossing all the x's for the love you save

hey who
hey who he
hey you
hey who you talkin' 'bout, me?
hey listen to me, hey listen to me, hey listen to me, hey listen to me
hey listen to me, hey listen to me, hey listen to me, hey listen to me
I got to say what I say
to say what I see, I say

I don't see what you say
coming straight out of me

hey I'm coming straight out of you
why don't you try on that shoe
try it on for size
might give you a rise

cause everything I said it, I said it cause I read it
& everything I said it, I said it cause I read it
& everything I said it, I said it cause I read it
& everything I said it, I said it cause I read it

gotta debunk all those trashy ideals
gotta reintegrate all the ideas you steal
"I understand" means I stand under yr heel . . .

woowie, hey man, you gotta light
because really I think yr getting just a little bit too heavy.
well I realize that. why don't you give me a break—& a half.
I could break yr arm. wouldn't do you any harm.
it's in the book, see. just take a look-see.
means what it says. says what it means.
"it's" only *it*. see what I *mean*
I mean to say. there's nothing to it.
the book's overdue. so go renew it.

sing a song w/ a rock'n'roll band
play the guitar w/ a feather in yr hand
but the feather would rather fly than be plugged in
& the poetry just has to be freed from the pen

gotta gumbo anarchistic sensibility
& I do not exclude those who reject me
sail the manic Titanic awash in the wine-dark sea
where the language is the water & the rocks are poetry

gotta riptide w/ all hands going down
into hot pants where the love runs aground
gotta whamma jamma lamma w/ the low-down meltdown core
gotta relax the wax, Max, to de-rug the floor
gotta rocket in my pocket that can sock it more & more

& the central calmness of my Being is predicated quite simply
in the act of Seeing both within & without in a remarkable fashion
to which one must remark as part of the act

gotta ROCK'N'ROLL MYTHOLOGY
gotta Total Apocalypse Pathology
got the most PostHysterical Poetry
& if it ain't coming at you then it's breezed on by

got the heavy-duty political intent
got the worm farm free-form diamond noodle content
I got breezy ways & boppin' rays
& when—hey, is this the end?
where it begins
ooo what a cheap shot
what a piece of cake shot

well. I suppose y'd rather leave it w/ a little downward trail
a demitasse of denouement to daily detail
not a bad idea in the kitchen making almond cakes & pies
what a pleasant surprise
go ahead & take a taste
one tiny slice
how nice

Veer

Took a chance and came here
Now your ear rustles on mine
Direct sound
"Language of Sleep" is the title
As soon as I go to sleep
Leaving quotation mark sentries
Protecting and lulling until
Falling asleep themselves. Good night.

5

VOLUME DIPS AND VARIABLE SPEEDS

FROM STEVE CANNON'S STOOP TO THE MITHRAIC PODIUM

Morocco Occo

Unbelievable to sit here whacked in Marrakech listening to young guide Mohammed's cassette which must be keeping everybody in the Hotel Chamel up and after *I'm* finished "listening" I'm to give it to the concierge, a skinny 18 year-old Ahmed with buzzburr haircut and scratch tenor voice that greets me each morning as I stumble to the john with "Ali Baba! Tarfaya! Sahara! Fatima!" commemorating my beard and my notion that the Moroccan Green March Army must've taken all the women (fatima) with them to Tarfaya, a Sahara outpost of which more later but at this time as far away as Timbuktu of which more later. And the cassette is "Jimi Hendrix" and I'm all ready to hash blast off into Outer Ladyland but no, wait—this is pop, it's rock, it's soul—it's "Rock Me Baby," remember, not by Jimi Hendrix, but—ready? *Eddie Kendricks.* O Morocco Occo! So *you* try telling this to Mohammed, who's dancing and humming and sudsing his mouth with your toothbrush and paste, a ritual he performs each time you settle into the hotel room. He shrugs. Laughs. He's listening to Jimi, or Eddie, or whoever you call him, music taped from an incredibly scratched record, little jumps that Mohammed anticipates as rhythms, volume dips and variable speeds, full of skips, slurs— "American music!" says Mohammed.

Not for Lack of Understanding

Have I come to you, nor from trying
To appease the habit of touch. This
Is not just to say, or talk myself over
A cliff, step step. Once I loved you

I couldn't be stopped, slapping the breakfast
Onto the floor & then kick it out the door
Down the stair out on the street. Just following
The little scrambled egg scraps washing downstream.

Nonintention Is Possible

A whole poem without love, square
On the death of Huey Newton, "in
A pool of blood," says *News*. Same day black
& white Orcas, giant Killer Whales,
Collide head on in a mission of power.
All-News Network shows footage
Of "Sea World, pool of blood." He
"[W]as caught," says *Times* editorial,
"Between the Book and the Street but could
Never escape the Street." Which is wrong.

Blood flowing in the arm is the Street,
Can you read it, the Book of the Street,
And what you don't like you turn the corner
Of that page. Men stand on that corner
Their lives away, racing round round
A dirty pool. The world cannot contain
The vision that encompasses the world

Such as Sweet Death finally opens the way,
Away from Life's brutalization. Oakland's
Black weather, intent on release, bang.

Censor Not

ensor not the oobly
            of yr doobly doo
Let it crown the crow
Grow a can of cow corn all shorn
For sure
It was the sea
Twas that the sea?

This Scratchy Life

No security, that's fine
No love, sure, sounds great
No blessing in disguise,
Or out of disguise either
That's good real goood
O! What a beautiful Absolute
Walking around, a beanbag of blood
Keeping pace with the air, a purple
Brilliance abop the brilliance
Because the poet tastes
The words as she makes 'em
The rules and roles are sweeping
Up is up wherever
The sea unfurls itself your hair
To make itself the sea

Words When Bored

Or it just comes out in the mix
All over the Midwest, they got
One good idea, but it's everybody

It's all in the mix in the Midwest,
And it's just one good idea,
But it deserves all the attention

Because I know who the enemy is
Being as I work in the advertising
And like it tight and weird

So let's get shipwrecked on a poem
Where poem fodder sustains
A party, us and all the dead writers

Just the ones we like: Dorothy Parker,
James Baldwin and Jane Bowles.
That's all literature, and I'll pull

The wool over the Midwest with the new
Monster Mix ad campaign if you hitch on
Another planet and swirl me right and

Call me everything, it's the sound
That drives me bonkos. I'm standing
Around sincerely off to the side as

Stop! The moon's a thief! you cry
Never stop telling me to stop
Swirling tight and weird and light

The One-in-a-Million Kid

It's the finger, Kid
It's the world
The world just gave you the finger, Kid
You go figure
Fuckin finger
Rows of 0's
The old goose egg, Kid
You been sittin on yr ass so long
It's so long, Kid,
Been good to know ya
You laid the golden goose egg, Kid
Sittin on the old goose egg,
The world just gave you a goose
What with all yr big zeros
Yr just blowin the nose of yr heros
Yr the one that's blowin it, Kid
It's right in front of yr face
But you won't face it, no
As plain as the face in yr face
Which it is always, Kid,
Always in yr face
Goose eggs with a finger, Kid
Go ahead, count em
There's 1,000,000 of em, Kid
Yr worth 1,000,000 to me, Kid
Yr the one, Kid, the one for me
Yr the one in 1,000,000, Kid

Future Love

I skid up to see her
Goo goo ya blues, Coco
Shake the shape & talk
It's all free, except you
Always pay & pay & then
      you pay
I've got a date, & guess
What, it's with you
Alarm is true, & I report
The bomb for you
It's a crime to rhyme
Truth with greed & capitalism
With a sense of purpose
I'm going to take your
Lovely sex & eat forever

A Quick Pound

Continual molds
Catch in your voice
Reflex aerial
Path of pathology
An active look as hawk
Beak extends into dove's throat
Break continuity here
Invent new language here
Commit suicide here
Transform into giant insect here
Eat buttered toast here
Make love here
Go back to work here

Suddenly it's not necessarily
The convenience of heart and lung
Same old story, up a cliff
Night the tide coming in
We'll never make it
Bite my lip
Dawn after dawn pours down

Etruscan Suns

You are alive.

And should hear the Truth
About yourself—I am a liar
Named the Sun—I am King of the Sun
And you are safe with me.

Life is complicated but sacred.
Nothing is Natural—just say
Goodby to the beautiful sky.
Look behind it and use the Bones.
For toothpicks. Inevitable
Errors lose all meaning.

Just to walk through the goats
To the gates! Mountains. Crickets.
Blue copper. A horse between
The pink mountains and . . .
Hold it! Behold the great
Rocks where the land howls!

There is nothing but green. Tunnels
Pierce the stones' hearts, small villages

Penetrate your desire. The wind
Makes your kind of scream. Listen.
This place will suit.
It has no foundation.

The Earth has a voice:
You can listen to cracked mud,
Still holding a flag. Surprise.
The world is bigger than your opinion.
Rome, a kiss on the brown horizon.
O poor desperate people, Love me!
For the walls of Rome have fallen,
The faces have been filled in, all Africa
Has been sacked to reveal pinnacles of fear
In your piazzas. Send gentle reports to the tombs.

Look at what the hillside reveals.
Gone are the quests, lawns and laws.
Now we will scream forever. St. Ivo's screws
Up a new sky. God's errors melt. What suspicion
Causes me to banish you? Only my
Daughters shall speak. Standing before
The gate late at night—

Dear Muse, bring me a party.
It is late, I am human, I am
Crying like children for their future.
What proverbs will succor now? Bring
Me more news, wicked and noisy. Cross
Black hopes with green sorrow.
I am Gold. Still the Sun's turning.

I'm a Boat. Take me.

Out of focus, a slender tear,
The final robe. Quick legs
To dust death. Come.
It is time for sleep.

Several Sonnets Later

Which map? This map
Which book? The other, please
Read fast. Then eat, you're
On TV.
Pull the covers
Up and motor across
The label with your legs
Crossed. Can you still
Panic as the century
Unforgivingly pulls
Its bow into its tie
As if the title ("Blue Snores")
Leads inevitably into
The whatchamacallit poem-type-thing:

So here's to you, amigo
And now it's back to me
I'll keep it a little while
Sort the mess and rack focus
More than never, more and less
A calm boost—the ensuing flap
I'll just keep the bird, thanks
You don't mind, you are
Lighting and brandishing the red cigar

There's an opera goin on in cell block Numero Cinque
Set in a small picturesque fishing village
Nicknamed "Fumicino," played by a sprawling
International airport who walks with a silver-
Headed cane, shape of a dog. . . .

The Italian Postal System

First all the envelopes are dipped.
For this purpose, giant scald cauldrons
Are used, the very ones that Caesar Augustus
Had ordered brought from Egypt for use as boneboilers
By the Capuchin monks. During the Dip
A strike probably occurs. The vats
Are then generally purged by all passing carabinieri
Whose uzis have been recently lost, but if not,
The steam, which has been clinging to the ever-
Changing ceiling frescoes, is revaporized
And thereafter recondensed several times by means
Of centrifugal coolants, with different centrifugal coolant
Manufacturers employed in the North, Central
And Southern Postal Universes. This process quite often replicates
The original addresses directly upon the appropriate
"Lost While In Transit" cards. Thus ends the Dip.

The donkeys are led out, and attached to the carts,
Each bearing the Postal Code Numbers, or, for International,
A System of Carrots, the sizes and expressive shapes
Of which have all been translated into a Code of the
World's Regions. Complex to the casual viewer, one
Italian family has been arranging these carrots
For centuries, and the Annual Festival of the Carrots,

Held in Gubbio but celebrated throughout Italy,
Is cause for great festivities in all branches of
The Postal System, and any letters in the carrot-ID'ed
Carts during this period (usually the month of July,
Occasionally extending into August or even September)
Are treated like good friends, i.e., never allowed to leave.
Many other elements, remnants of previous Postal
Systems, abound, with meanings lost in time but which
Still provide glimmers of the ancient ways, and for many
Are, indeed, a palimpsest of life itself. That
The whole actually functions, and that one can,
By placing one's tongue directly on the tiny wafer-
Like stamp, actually participate in this oldest
Of rituals, is a miracle open to everyone.

A Visitation by John Belushi on the Isle of Capri

Constant eating   Constant motion
We watched videos but only his videos
He gave a running commentary, a sort of gag-by-gag
Play-by-play: analytic and complete—imagine
"Animal House" with gesticular footnotes. He dubbed it
"Ye Olde Eternal Classic," although I couldn't quite make
That out just then, seeing as how I was totally preoccupied
With rolling on the floor at the time. I was not alone
In laughing, however; indeed, it was John's laugh itself
That transmitted to me, immediately and wholly, his entire
Comic Cosmic Theory, looking directly down and through
The clear Caprian Mediterranean blue suddenly coming
Face-to-face with the face behind the mask of Comedy.
His laugh functioned like a strange chemical, causing all substance

To diffuse at once into its parts, while simultaneously taking on
A physical appearance of nothing less than a sheet of gold,
Which again, as it slowly lifted, revealed, and directly implanted,
The True and Complete Nature of Humor According to Belushi.
At this precise moment of revelling revelation, I was able to gasp
Just enough air between laughter-rapture convulsions to blurt out
"All comedy is a yearning!" a statement which stopped time dead.
It happened like this: a quick hitch in John's eyebrows,
Confucius's pivot on the wobble, and then an odd wind
Rustled a few hairs on my arm: the congruent pause
Stretched Infinity. Whew. Like a balloon,
John ultimately burst into gales of hilarity, veils of relief,
Seems I'd just delivered the punchline to end
All punchlines, the Ultimate Topper, and his antics
Certainly proved contagious, so much so that we were now
Both rolling, Pigs in Heat, yet another movie,
We were sweating Giant Turtles. Unfortunately, our cavorting
Couldn't help but eventually awaken my family—the four of us,
Five counting John, were staying in a small room
In a small hotel, the Belsito. Capri itself is quite
Dear, quite touristy, and yet somehow quite charming and,
Indeed, quite beautiful: we were fond of saying that somehow
They had not been able to mess it up yet, all of which
Made Belushi think of la bella isola as "somehow appropriate
For an appearance of this kind," the complete
Absurdity of which sent us guffawing straight
Into the bathroom, prodded as we were by the sleepy regalings
Of my poor family, who, thank God, must have been dreaming
That they themselves were the ones having the darn strangest
Dreams! as we shut the door and shushed each other, trying to hold
Our laughs in, listening at the door as best we could
To the deep breaths of my loved ones as they assumed

The absolute rhythms of sleep, a song which in turn
Signalled sighs and exhalations between the two of us.

And so we were hanging in the bathroom—here,
Things became a bit more somber. Indeed, we cried.
Light began filtering in, that peculiar light red
Gold light of Capri they say "touches the skin."
"My folks were from Napoli," John was saying, and in the light
I saw him smiling far away as he remembered, "They always
Thought Capri a real hoot." As far as youth goes, and college-
Type humor, John had a heart attack right then and there, like
"Time for work," gagged with a spoon, way dead.
In the bathroom we discuss philosophy was another
Belushi-ism clincher. By this time John was doing heart attack
After heart attack, blue and brilliant, fibrillating all over
The swirling yellow and white tiles. The bidet kept
Getting in the way, but then I saw, he was using
The bidet! Twas an all-new Belushi, attuned
To women in a model modern male way . . . But no politics,
Puleeze!
Back to the puerile! To-Ga! he'd shriek—that classic refrain,
Rendered all the more poignant from atop the toilet can cover.
Suddenly he stopped, laurels sliding down over his brow,
And said he'd seen my daughters earlier that night
At the piazzetta, running through the legs of the macho ragazzi,
Busting their cool. That was fantastic, he whispered, looking off.
It's a lot of tough yuks, really, he continued musing, serious
Giggles under the toga. And as for you, and your job, which
Was the next topic he veered into, his gaze blazing at me,
You're a poet, what a riot! And just Righteous enough! he allowed,
Like a priest at a well. At this point he drew himself up
And started in poeticizing, a la Kovacs' Dovetonsils, brilliantly

Satirical improvisations, accompanied by a little dancing.
"What a rapper!" I was about to remark, when again he abruptly
Stopped and, freezing like a statue, appealed, "But hush,"
And I saw that the room was filled to bursting by the light,
Dusty apples of April dawn, the girls laughing in their sleep,
My wife's beauty peeping out from beneath the sheets—
"It's time! Time to get out of the bathroom!"

These words had great meaning, and thus we did, we did
Get out of the bathroom, rest easy. But before we did,
John did an extraordinary thing, or rather, his head did.
I remember this moment crystal-etched: John's looking at me
So beautifully, with an all-embracing, all-loving look,
As his voice simply continued on about this and that. And the reason
Why, Dear Reader, I happen to remember all this so very clearly
Is simply because what happened next was the most astonishing
Image of my life, giving purpose not only to this visitation,
But also to my entire life from that moment on. For it was then,
Accompanied by a peculiar whirring hum, that the top
Of John's head, from right above his ears and thence straight across
His forehead, began to revolve. His hair line became a blur
As it began spinning round, picking up speed. The low hum,
A drone behind his words, and the sounds of the words themselves
Began to abstract and fly around, not unlike his hair,
Although the meanings of the words remained clear, meanings
That were now alternating between deep tones of tragedy
And high peals of comedy, meanings that picked up resonance
As the twirling head picked up speed, meanings that became
A language so direct as to not require the act of comprehension,
Instead becoming a simple link, a connecting sine wave of emotion
That was at once totally strange and totally comforting
And for which words can only desperately attempt to describe.

The drone began a slow crescendo, my eyes remaining glued
To John's spinning dome: the pure Motion of Revolution.
And it was at this epiphanous moment that a sudden burst of light
Quite literally blinded me, causing the surrounding whirling noise,
With cascading fury, to become all, all, and all,
A frenzied cyclone of noise, a noise which, as my sight slowly
Returned, and focus turned to Sense, I could actually see:
Silver and liquid and pouring down a slender funnel
Directly into John's skull, for as I watched, mesmerized,
The whirling third portion of his head began to lift off and reveal,
But *No-o-o,*
It was not a spinning ball of gold,
Instead it was blue and green and sweet,
As the world itself grew out of John's skull
And I followed it outside the bathroom and so back to sleep.

Dreams: Roma

NIGHT

> Just a wind blows
> Against the palaster
> Picks up the landscape
> Tree by tree dragging
> Boulders and dreaming
> Civilization comes running

EQUAL SHADOWS

> A figure in the doorway
> She is as by a mountain
> But crumples, still divine,
> Not back to humans

Let them stay
Pigs using only English
Pushing the rock up
To ascertain that
The inscription
Makes no sense

YOU KNOW MY SECRETS

They killed their husbands
So they must draw water
From the cistern in dippers
With sieve bottoms and carry
As water drips out step
By step—more about
This later, this frustration
More about this frustration
Than the crime. More later.

Dreams: San Sepolcro

FIGURE IN DOORWAY

Crystal morning
Bells rock the jack
No more ear
Than music, ever
As night collects
In the folds of time

HAND TO MOUTH

Ah, I am stopped short

Red beauty. I'll tell
You about the figure in
The doorway—it was you.
The police and box after box
Of green peppers, beautiful green
Peppers. You know my secrets,
You make my dreams. The space
Between the doorframe
And the single figure
Intuits the group, society,
Civilization. But hand
To mouth gesture, framed
Proximity forever, age chips out
The back wall, sweet time down
The long hall forever waiting.

Pay Per View

True Romans now eat and pay
Per view—best in the world,
High atop the Zodiac, ancient
Streets tumble loopity down Gianicolo
Towards San Lorenzo Cemetery,
Just cross town, as the pious
Or lapsed or totally heathen constantly
Do, sucking the blood from the orange
As the days last forever and you never
Die. Perhaps, but then again, and as
The red lips grasp the language,
Light breeze picks up again, words kite
Fresh and clear, a meaning arising from

3000 year swamp, daily routine. Certainly
You may have my wallet, I was growing
Too attached to my beard, sad for
No reason am I crying this tear?

It's not history, but it's all that's left
Of it, a parachute glimpsed
From the corner of your eye
From the corner of the piazza. To sit,
Yes, in the shade with the congenial
News always lashing the perspective
To the bar where a lone soul is stirring
Sugar into a tiny cup while mobs line up
At the cash to give over everything for
A slip of paper to be torn in translation.

Maybe you've never been here, but you
Certainly pointed in this direction. The music
Is opera, and not that easy to dance to,
But under the moon the statues do come
Alive, revealing that they are us and always
Have been, with grace and ease and all
The other attributes that keep us up nights,
Ferociously biting each other and staying hungry.

There Is No Dog

All the Futurists
Sit at the table talking
About propellers we
Interrupt then I'm afraid
You're caught a flash

Bulb pop pass the salt
Cross the generations the sea

Marinetti, prowling Porta Portense
Insists on doubling the asking prices
Not enough lira, he cries
In the whole damn world!
And Belli, the devil genius,
He order Fascist this and Fascist
That. The sun never rises. Trastevere
Is next, a round of amaros, then
Another round. The music swirls,
A Roman candle swells, Ste. Maria
Gelato bongs her golden bells—
Hear the bells Hear the bells
What do they say
You're in Rome You're in Rome
Come outside and play

Tears of Futurists, now, Amici,
It's been many years of darkness
And one more dinner before
No more breakfast before we
Awake the portiere at the Etruscan
Museum, climb into the tombs,
For a nonperformance, the audience thus
Divided into two camps begins
Quietly shouting Lights Lights
Which in the blackness is all too clear
As we come to life, shrouding life,
Shouting Lights Lights Lights
Rock the tombs

Rare and Beautiful Things at Half-Price

It is 1991
It is remarkable
It is rare and beautiful
And of course it is on sale

It's a red light that means go
If you honk and it's a green light
That means kill the Kurds and it's
A yellow light that blinks longingly and means
Nothing at all

Perhaps it is time
For a reassessment
While 1000s die
And a time for a new
Way of learning
Why the act of breathing
Means somebody dies

Please explain the legal hierarchy
To the criminal beaten at your feet
Build a better box
With more sides
And make it smaller and smaller
As you use your body for a marker
Holding down the parking space
For the fully-equipped and luxury-appointed

Once there was a life
Now you are a hospital
Born of a teenager
That's why I'm the way I'm so bad and wild

The Ideal City

What blue child serious and deadly
Sits above the moon to judge the world
Only a madman would scrim the truth
Knock the wind out of the bourgeoisie
And still find someone to pay for it

It's the Ideal City, above heaven itself
Hills and mountains hidden by the round strength
I cried there, between the wells so perfectly balanced
Silver porches and slender silent gusts
This was protection, a small golden light
And a glass detail sweep the marble piazza

No Dream

Went down to the shop
Like every morning—wearing
My red suit—strange
Old woman comes in—all
I remember. Next a family,
I'm the papa, I don't
Recognize them. They're
Breaking down our door
I wrote the wrong door
The angels won't let us use
The ladders I climb anyway
The moon translates—See me
Pinned down there with love
And dependence. Thus I
Sleep at last with my own

Family, all dressed in red.
Demons guard our feet,
Angels our head.

Poem 3/2

There's No Big Message except hope you've had a good time
While reading this

While somewhere the Great Novel is being shredded
I must stand up and say my piece
Or at least a piece of my piece "Shredded Piece"

I will never sit in that class again, a stone
Eating away at the heart of existence

Plenty of homeless people want to read my poems
They are lucky I stand at the newsstand
Cursing the politicians and making faces

Maybe all I'm saying is it's a real job
Being unemployed

Penis Envy in Saudi Arabia

Buncha soldiers sit around talkin

One guy says to the other
Wish I had *yr* penis
Other guy says, What is this,
some kind of joke?
We're livin in a joke,

says another guy
But the pay's ok,
another guy speaks up
I've got it, let's all
trade penises, the first guy says
Back home they respect us
& our penises, another guy nods
Hey guys, a young recruit chimes in,
I don't even *have* a penis
& I don't want one, so just put
yr peckers back in yr pants &
let's get back to work, ok?

With a muffled shuffle all the
genitalia are returned.
Damn, one guy mutters, that horizon
sure is a long ways off

For the Birds

The Birds are whispering
Tweets into my ears
Tweet tweet
Tweet tweet
I must be a Saint
St. All of a Sudden

What are they tweeting?
That is between
Me and the Birds

Now I am in The Birds
And they are in me
They are dive-bombing me
They seem no longer
To regard me as saint
And I seem to be running
As St. Alfred Lord Hitchcock
Screams out "Cut! Cut!"

However the Birds are not cutting
They are not whispering Tweets anymore either
They are slicing and diving
And I am running across the desert

Is it because I would not tell my own people
The secrets of the Birds?
Who are my people, anyway, I ponder
Now that I am movie star

As I stumble on in the desert
Upon the answers I receive
Divine illumination and I see
Tiny insects swarm round the heads
Of the Birds that swarm round me
Tiny insects dive-bomb Birds
Birds dive-bomb me

I can no longer translate
Tweet tweet into Bzz bzz
Why do you hate me so
I wrote this in the movies

Even in the dark these thoughts
Do not stop dive-bombing
It is dark here
It is hard to write in the dark
It is hard to think in the dark
The bombing outside takes on a steady rhythm
As I pull down my mask, get runway clearance
And take off with my babies under my wings
Claws extended, bill open and screaming
Tweet tweet

Good to Hear from You

to Gregory Kolovakos

A wise person once said these words
And you expect me to repeat them? Never,
For in that repetition there is is something
Gained in the translation? Always. Never
Say no to anything, and in that way it'll take
Care of itself. When it is the world, you'll
Understand why it feels better when someone else
Does it. A brave new noun sits down and gently
Whispers, "Never you mind," like the P.E. teacher's
Wife in *The Last Picture Show.* Your memorial went

As well as could be expected, Gregory, without
You there. People are still talking. The violinist
Cried, the jackhammer in the street peppered the air.
The floral arrangements under the electric fan shook
        like a hurricane.

Poetry
Balance

Yo Bimbo
Bimbo Rivas
Yo this and that
Balance with Eternity
Just for a little while

Holman   Bob

The Irony of the Ecstasy

In the bank I certify that I
Am I to get the money out
To give the lawyers to send
To Miguel to get the building back

Cecilio. He comes in. Quick time zip
Chinese New Year's, the firecrackers like
His birth, and now he's grown, helping Miguel,
Who's running out of gas, faster than I

Can write the poem. Well, that is typical,
As the bank purrs, and spring turns
Into new dough, smelling yeasty, Russian
Baths, Cecilio adrift, the blackened loaf

98

Is handed over, the goods, just as the Bronx
Bomber (Miguel's '72 Caddy) drinks its last,
And contentedly expires the tires. Hotfooting
Down Canal for fuel, we talk fund-raising, state

Agencies, see belt-tightening low-tech poets,
Spend money to make poetry, huh, pipe
Dreams, plumbing realities. New York flashes
Emergency as Café reemerges, ecstasy's haven.

Underdose o' Café

4/17/92

Well Frank Burt
wrote a soggy napkin
"The image of some imagined
nonthing somehow thingable"

I rolled it round
a lifesaving sweetness
3am Nuyorican
till the vitamins split

Then I surfaced
as he was saying
"shrouded in this gentle slag"

I'm on To Twell the Twooth!
Synchronicity vs. Poetry
cept ain't no vs.
with us.

La Petite Punaise dans le Bassinet

(LITTLE BEDBUG IN THE BASSINET)

"Never surrender the love zap!"

The floor is the first shelf
And natural savagery
Gets you where you
Want to go
When you're seven days old

Little Dipper

Now cry. Now eat. Now pee. Now now.
You say, I hear. Now sleep.
And see with. What you say,
Baby, the day's eye to see
Baby, what do you see? Dream
Crisis begets new address. Dream
You can't bring it with you: Housing

You can't bring it with you. Housing
Crisis begets new address: Dream
Baby, what do you see? Dream
Baby, the day's eye to see
And see with. What you say
You say, I hear. Now sleep.
Now cry. Now eat. Now pee. Now now.

The Tent Hath Grown

Oh Lordy, I'm so full of stories, you
Just try and shut me up in this tent.

Why, when I first climbed up these Rocky
Peaks, some eight years or so ago, and set
My beer bottle down and let the wind blow
Across, resonating a lullabye, we had a
Smallish tent, barely room for my wife-
To-be, and me, and our chaperone. Now I sit
Alone, keeping an eye on el tento grande,
Big enough for her and me and the two who've
Come along and matured so delicately in
The interim, little wildflowers, sown here
On the scorched ground looking for life,
And I, as the ancient farmer driving the pick-
Up replied to his wife's query concerning
The growing distance between them ("We used
To sit so close together"), "I ain't moved."

These mountains still stun, mocking the poem.
In *USA Today,* weather passes for news, but I
Still can't keep up with it.
                          The clouds progress
Over the Tetons, elders at their grandchildren's
Graduation. I read with fascination about Detroit
City's new poetry. Is there anything else? It's
Windy, I'm concerned that the tent stay put or blow
Off with me in it. Tomorrow it's Montana. Whoopi-ti.
A morsel for some grizzly. A landing base for a fly.

Crow's Big as a Bog

Deer larks like a log
Who cuts the grass in the forest
Who built the lodge I found the remains

Many moons ago, I did
I ripped the phone out of the plane tree
It was loud and insistent but could not
Awake the owl
Who sleeps beside me sometimes

My TV Poem

Holding my nose,
I write TV Poem

Why write it down in books
Make big stink
Everything gets all stinky
& it's all my fault

I got in your space
TV is my face
I am the only person
In the world

Birthday Morning, 1991

Elizabeth

First thing wake up
Look out window
Write poem beginning
"There is no window . . ."

So you think there is no light.
Light plays in a hollow place.
To face one face with so many legs,
Try them all in a single embrace.

This one's childish, this adultish,
Delicious, coltish . . . Smoothing
The forehead from sleep's foolish
Palette, waking up dancing together.

Wow. Yeah. C'mon Baby
Wake up and dance with me.

30 Minutes

Into 39 I pause & take a break
To toss these passing thoughts like
Leaves into great salad. Like life
At 30 minutes, Sophie was whisked
Into Intensive Care, my mother's
Mother died in childbirth, and *Truth
Or Consequences,* no I take it back,
The Price Is Right, today became
The Longest-Running Half-hour in the
History of Recorded Time. I'll sit
On this, you stand around, & that's
The way it is, 12:36 am, 10 March 1987.

Night House

The wind of 6th Ave kicks in

The lavish kite unscrolls
An ancient tale of love
And treachery

It's just one of those Nights

So tired from working
That you can't sleep

And it isn't even funny
As the pen clenches
Your fingers to its end

Life can be like that
One minute
You're running
Around and then
The next you're lying
Still next
To the one
You love

Sure it happens
All the time

Cats asleep
On the sofa, kids
In bunkbeds

Me too
Real soon
Me too

No Longer Killing Mosquitos

Once, a million years ago, on LSD
I was sitting underneath a "you" tree
On top of a mountain overlooking a lake

The whole gang was tripping and we

Were doing the exploring nature thing—
I was writing how the "they" become
An "us" under the yew
            And as I was
Working on the poem, I could feel
The "Hurry up! Where's Bob?" vibe
Of Group Consensus closing in on
Me, as I to Us by Them
Was being called to join in
Crashing down the mountain
To those Other Rituals like:
    Metaphysical Pool
    Make movie sans camera of First Man Arising From Lake Depths
And the Ultimate:
    Get in a Car and Go
For a drive and see if you can figure out which of the kaleidoscoping
Roads is "real." But first: the Poem Must End
For as the group noose circled me in,
A mosquito landed on my left arm (I am writing
Right-handed, now as then) and as I observed
My own blood entering the proboscis protuberance
The human buzz became so intense
I slapped that mosquito flat into the page
Splattered blood, the final period
As they became us
Part 2—Today heavenly, above Lake Canandaigua,
Twenty-two years later, far from madding, no drugs, I sit
In a spot of nature and write this poem.
Sit on a downed lodgepole pine, some calcified droppings
By my feet—bear's? or human's? From the scat I carefully
Extract, using my pen, the carcass of a Daddy Longlegs
And watch as an ant carries it off. A caterpillar

Wriggles over my pants, and again with pen
I lift it off and transport it, dangling,
To new oak leaf. At home, West 12th Street,
10014, my daughters are just getting back from school.
Elizabeth and I have been married 11 years.
I am writer-in-residence here at Gell House,
Finger Lakes. I am perched out behind
The hidden cabin, just above the tombstone
Of the Gells. When mosquitos land,
I wave them gently on their way.

A tiny flash, no thing reverses

A field green blue field
My father's blue wide white eyes
He is breathing through his eyes of death
A mountain over his heart just stays there
A tiny gray field, my father's tiny head
Our slow car crosses a bridge
Children at play dash
To the sides of the bridge
"Someday you will play like that Robert"
I will play like them in the field of death
Fences cut wheat
Sun fades wet into dark
I cross the bridge alone as it dissolves
Thunder pulls my heart into my father's eyes
Blue and wide and inside skin
Mother mother where have you been
I've been out back to Pineville town
I've walked the mountain all around
Robert, you will play like them
In the fields of men and women

6
I CAN'T BELIEVE IT'S NOT A POEM!

The Death of Poetry

It sucked itself into the coffin spasm
It was no beauty there
It was enforced tradition of emptiness
The newspaper of truth did not exist

A table with six learned peoples
Read the leftovers for the Monday night crowd
Pick up the pay like any other worker
How was anybody to know?

Sure I sit on the ledge
And keep my feet in midair
You in your whiny highchairs
Think us as Disappeared

A thing or two perhaps like your eyes
Make It New fr chrissake it snaps
Your vision's elasticity cracks
Make It New Language no habla ingles

Nobody came to the Death of Poetry
Musta happened long long time ago
Musta been forgotten dream uninterpreted
As your hand shovels at your funeral

I had a dream but who wouldn't
Casually tossing the modalities of Milton
Hey, amigos, let's go for it public swoon
The starving people, still digging for sustenance

Missionary Epistle

I was just sitting down
When the world blew up
When the gun burped
When the bald guy's head blew off

And you can't usurp the poem
The power of the seemingly
The so-called forget-about-it meaningless
Beauty of beauty thing poem

That dashes the hopes of the dogmen
And lies in wait at supermarket checkout counters
And is broadcast so live it's skin

I was kissing my daughter when my heart
Pounded right out of my body
I was seeing double, the Future was only part
I was no longer panicked
The streets were read

Jazz was the anthem and a big box
Had enough lunch for the world
There was no more teaching and Who Cares
Was not a put down

Because you didn't have to care
Things cared for you

And guess what, I'm a bitter failure
Baking flour into lives and a nutritious
Momentary collapse is all I ask for

So translate these whistles of spit
Whipping through the airless void
And bring back Life itself,
You, Missionary of Chaos and Joy

1990

The taking of flash photos & use of recording devices of any kind,
including pens, pencils, eyes & ears, is strictly encouraged.

It's 1990
& Nelson Mandela is free!

& people are looking at each other
They're going like "Wha?"
& the other people are looking back
& they're going like "Duh?"
& finally, after this deep interaction,
You hear the wild cry of:
"Excuse me, could you tell me the time?"

What time is it?
It's Wake & Shake Time
It's Death of the Decade Time
It's Turn of the Century Time
It's Gyrate the Millennium Time

It's the End of Time
"At the sound of the tone it will be the End of Time"
It's 1 PF—it's post future
It's 1 PT—it's post time
It's Post Time!

It's 1990
& Nelson Mandela is free!

History's on fast forward
Make that double-fast fast forward
That's where you run past the Future so fast you're back in the Past
Sure, it's the End of History
So how come all we can think is, "What comes next?"
One minute you're rolling in ecstasy because the Berlin Wall is
     tumbling down,
The next you think, a reunited Germany! Oh God no!
Here come the storm troopers! & I'm Jewish (Well, my father was
     Jewish, so I'm not Jewish enough for the Jews—but I'm
     Jewish enough for the Nazis!)
One minute it's survival tactics & the next it's where's the angle

It's 1990
& Nelson Mandela is free!

& everybody wants a little glasnost
We know we want it cause we see Frank Zappa smoking cigarettes
     with Vaclav Havel, who 6 months ago was in jail, an artist
     whose work was banned by the government, now he's the
     President of Czechoslovakia
So stop in for free baby burritos at the corner bar
Except suddenly it's a karaoke sushi bar specializing in piranha sushi,
     & everybody here's a star,

110

Because you get to stand in front of the massive TV screen showing
   an MTV-minus one video clip & sing along with the bouncing
   ball—
Except the words are all in Japanese and how can you sing "Feelings"
   with feeling in Japanese?
Kanjiru! Watashiwa, kanjiru!

It's 1990
& Nelson Mandela is free!

Communism has collapsed
At last the Russians get to wear the "Happy Face" masks & stand in
   line for a Beeg Mek
The Azerbaijanis are finally free so they get to beat up on the
   Armenians
Yugoslavia has decided to go back to indigenous cave tribe groupings
In Italy the Communists have met & decided they're not
   Communists
They're gonna change their name to be more appealing to the
   Socialists and the Greens
But for the time being they're calling themselves simply The Thing
The Thing! Personally, I'm planning to vote for—the Thing
For the time being   For the time being
There's nothing left anymore except for the time being
You live your whole life for the time being
While meanwhile—there is no meanwhile

It's 1990
& Nelson Mandela is free!

"Play ethics by ear"
Let me out of here—but which way is out?
I'm a part of the *food chain,* isn't that enough?

111

At night I snuggle up close to the warm blue glow of images
     provided for everyone by a select few
Listen, they've packaged a shopping mall so small you can only visit
     it with a Video Walkperson, a cellular phone and a Visa card
The world is changing, but we're not
We're stuck in a commercial for Life
Trying to figure out who to give the money to
When, surprise! There is no money

It's 1990
& Nelson Mandela is free!

Señor Yuppie! Phone call for Señor Yuppie!
Pardon me, have to step over these homeless people to close on my
     Home Equity Loan, sorry
"Our bodies are still tender & not full grown & the prospect of
     dying frightens us all, but history calls us & we must go"
But where did they go, the Chinese students on their bicycles riding
     towards the tanks at Tiananmen Square?
It can't happen here because it's already happened here
AIDS epidemic grabs Life till we don't even see it, gone like holes
     in heart,
Surrounded by ghosts, meeting Death in the middle of Life
While lesbians and gay men still have to fight for the right to love
& be sure to send your poetry to the Department of Official Bullshit
     to get labelled
So it just has to be—time to get a Co-op!—
     buy the place you used to rent, and still get to pay the rent
It's time to be a great parent—
     work extra hours to pay for the best childcare while you're
     away
My kid is majoring in Nikes

Don't worry! Don't be happy! Explode!
The decision of birth from her body is solely & privately that of the
    woman herself

It's 1990
& Nelson Mandela is free!

And everything used to be something else
Now it's *1,000* words a minute, & Times Square is just so much
    more interesting
We're hellbent on something, sort of positive in a senile way
I can't even keep up with my life
It's a secret between me & my stunt double
Honey, I'm home—nuke me
Hop to it, ban cigarettes before it's too late
It's Earth Day again, if you can find any earth left
Paranoia used to be a psychosis, now it's a national pastime
Try the new fashion: the bare breast style of no clothes at all, & it's
    not cheap, either
& poetry is the newspaper of the future
Except it's locked out of the media
You know things! Think them!
There's optimism at the yacht club
The salad bar is open
Excuse me, isn't it time to mow your head?
I hate you! Thank you very much, have a nice day
They don't even know what it is, but they've already got an option
    on it
They're buying into it! Let's Not Make A Deal!

It's 1990
& Nelson Mandela is free!

& there's a guy at the microphone & he's yelling at me
& he's not using language that makes any sense from where I come
   from
It all rhymes & it all starts with capital letters
& it's all intense italics underlined three times in bold face headlines
& all I can remember is the part about
It's 1990
& Nelson Mandela is free!

& around the world a sense of possibility
As women slowly ease the old gray dinosaur poobahs from their
   penile thrones
The universal remote control is being passed into your hands

Zap it! Zap it!
Zap it! Zap it! Zap it!

It's 1990
& Nelson Mandela is free!

How to Wake Up

1. Go to sleep

One Way of Looking at a Blackbird

That is no blackbird
That is a window
And a little tiny brick

10 Things I Do Every Day

Suicide

DisClaimer

As Dr. Willie used to say,
We are gathered here today
because we are not gathered
somewhere else today, and
we don't know what we're doing
so you do—the Purpose of SLAM!
being to fill your hungry ears
with Nutritious Sound/Meaning Constructs,
Space Shots into Consciousness
known hereafter as Poems, and
not to provide a Last Toehold
for Dying Free Enterprise Fuck 'em
for a Buck'em Capitalism'em. We disdain
competition and its ally war
and are fighting for our lives
and the spinning
of poetry's cocoon of action
in your dailiness. We refuse
to meld the contradictions but
will always walk the razor
for your love. "The best poet
always loses" is no truism of SLAM!
but is something for you
to take home with you like an image
of a giant condor leering over
a salty rock. Yes, we must destroy
ourselves in the constant
reformation that is this very moment,
and propel you to write the poems
as the poets read them, urge you

to rate the judges as they trudge
to their solitary and lonely numbers,
and bid you dance or die between sets.

What You Can't Understand Is Poetry
Is Connected to the Body Again

Jean allowed the body to drop
The beautiful face bluing so perfect
A fly buzzed by—but no one would believe it
She raced frantically to the offices of the *National Enquirer*
A reporter wrote up the story—it made the cover
Now she could get the attention of the radical newsweekly
That only told the truth
She just casually flipped it down on the desk
"Hey," an editor reading upside-down said,
"What if this story is true? It would certainly change
Our story—maybe we should look into this.
Hey! *Stop those presses!*"

Jean walked away. Horns were blaring,
It was a brilliant dusty sunset and the sirens were distorting.
She didn't hear 'em.
She was remembering her lover's face,
What they'd said about how you never know
If someone else's orgasm is better than yours
But that shouldn't stop you
From coming together
Even if it's not exactly
At the same time.

Head of Kovacs

Funny is the man whose mind goes
Places where the wild shows
Fun show hip throw way to go yo
Spring sprang a leak at the Joke Boutique
Whom done it to the max? // Ernie Kovacs

The master / of the faster past
The poobah / of the future blast
Kovacs. Kovacs? Co-opt cosine co-rain co-shine
It's // Ernie Kovacs Time.

The matter doesn't matter
& the facts aren't straight
& the Late Show? Sorry, it's just too late
No humdrum rerun oh no

Makin crazy crazy—& hipper'n hip
No psychedelic relic talkin roundtrip
What became the legend most?
The legendary host // Ernie Kovacs

Mustard the dog—barkin the socks
Poet in the kitchen—let's rock rock rock
Wilder'n wild
Cooler'n cool
Behind the owl mind
The kick of a mule
There's no myopia
In my utopia

117

Gig the wig wax the facts & a mighty high ho
"Honey, what's the name of The Ernie Kovacs Show?"

A gelatine skeleton of In-no-sense
Personifies the Pratfalls of Intelligence
Makes you laugh out loud
Be a singular crowd
A hit of a wit & a fun of a gun
You're the target so you better run
Or don't. You're in it
Come on, let's begin it
Don't blink without it
Think about it
Whom done it
He begun it

Unite tonight
In dead black & white
Ernie Kovacs Show-show
TV-a-gogo

A POEM FOR NEAL CASSADY, CALLED SIMPLY,

Neal Cassady, Thinking He Is Hanging from His Fingertips over the Great Abyss, Is in Fact Slipping Slowly into the Smokestack of a Giant Steam Locomotive

I no fear
What am I doing here
Jest a glance in the chance dance
Of the mirrored rearword

118

Fresh burnt freak free to see
Jaybirds runnin naked outta the burbs
Shoutin how's life's a blurb for itself!
Verb don't be, man, 's'a cat
Catapult o' nine tales
Flailin sails on the rat re-rated nation eviscerated
Nickel 'n' dime free view preview
Meet my Dad's Shinycheese, my Mom's Arabars
My grandparents came from Venus MalloMars
My brothers and sisters alive inside my blisters
And I keep track of the stars, that's my job
To keep track of the dovetails,
    the exhausted pipes,
        and the stars

Don't eat meat, don't swallow greens
All's I eat is air'n'hair'n'beans
Keep myself rolling steam in a dreamroller
Steamroller rolling a dream flat'n
Wilco the echo, Fernononononono
Good season two good reason to believe'n
Look to your left to see right through
This skinna mine sure wants skin offa you

Did the impolite o'liticalical imp slip the spine slime?
Fracture jaw gewgaw dunky can o'hide?
See it breathe it leave it sneeze it freeze it
60 miles a second to get laid in LA
Juice caboose laying life tracks for home
Come livvylivvylive at springtime's bone

Wake me when I'm dead

119

Shoulda fucked my own mind instead
Why bother why not
Why bother why not
Why bother why not

Just a prairie dog and a full dictionary
Discretely dishing the head vitamins' vision
Type hype for a finish sans blemish
Or leave the spittle in the middle—open your openings
The man in the moon I prune
The enjine whines and the tall pines pine
For all's I love's a dove above
'n a particular fuse o' you
Ivy grows over me own tomb's tone
Firmly entrenched
Right here on this bench
I'm Quetzalcoatl, I'm Welch, lynched
Shook a tale farther, Quetzaltototl
I'm not, I'm a knot o' snot
And I'm fallin, I'm fallin
I'm fallin fallin fallin
What's next on the way
On the way?
Andale!
We're on delay?
We're on hold
I ain't on hold
I'll hold the cold
I'll tell the told, freak the fold, bend the bold
But I'll be rolled if I'll hold on hold

No second thoughts thanks
The first one's overdone
With a *wait a second!* second
As another one's begun

It's just your mind's startin to dovetail
And the exhasted pipe's on the third rail
Sloogging through the swampy swampy night
Frozen on a cruisin loosin sight
Goin blind in a minute for a dollar bill pill
Down on the ground poundin reality till
The whole picture frameup slaps the fine on fine
I'm *having* a nice day thank you suiciding the line
Up the damn down into the sound of the sound
Where death lights the match to catch a snatch o'
What the blurred word inferred implied
On the high time tide
Instant reincarnation—tongue to ear resuscitation
The rattlin battlin of mouth ear, Mouthear
Come near come near come near
Come here come here come here
Come hear my fear

57 Gazillion Lung-Tongue Varieties

for Bob Carroll

Hey, US!
Get up!
Stand up!

Pay up
The Bill of Writes!

Hey, Poets!
Time to fill up
Swirling Void Hole
At empty center
Of National Consciousness Doughnut!

Our Whole's got a hole in it!
From which the Soul of the Nation is leaking—

Hey, US!
It's time to Re-soul!

Poets of the World, re-write!
Rewrite History as
        57 Gazillion
                Lung-Tongue
                        Varieties

Crack the dazed,
        The bored
                The goofed-off with

The dazzling,
        The bo*ring* as in "Laser-zap*ping*,"
Collaborative, co-conspiritorial
Chchch turn the beat around
And stick to it, Love Magnet!

I will now read you your 1st Amendment Writes, to wit:
                "This imminently transferrable,

122

Readily assumable Poetic License
Is yours immediately free-for-all,
But—
You gotta speak it up to keep it up!
You have the Right to Noisy!"

(Uh, I don't uh really unnerstand. What is *it,* exactly?)

       "Tag, *you* are *it!*"

Japan's annual Tree Poem celebration of
Everybody writes Tree Poems.
Tree Poem seeds, planted in brains,
Nurtured through arborious fertilizing rituals.
Citizens read "Trees in Poems' Breeze,"
Chchch returning leaves to trees they sprang from.

In US,
We sing rock'n'opera in the shower.
Who's all wet?

This just in: News Bullet-in,
Name of country chchchchanges
To United States of Poetry!
Creates CD-ROM instaccess to Who We Are!
Physicallizes First Amendment Rites!
Guarantees Po-for-All! 57 Gazillion Varieties
Of newly-free voices raised as one
From top shelves of Dust Museums!

Poets of the US, Rewrite!
You have nothing to lose but your place in line
At the Unified Lifetime Checkout Counter

What do you pick? Quick!
Pick your brains!

And when the poetry reading is over
We sit round the campfire, Australopithecus's Television,
And have an Open Mic,
Where we open up Mike and she says,
Not in the shower but to showering stars,

> *Molecules free*
> *To be you and me*

And when we run out of poems
The conclusive Emily XYZ
Borrows a twenty-dollar bill and tags *it,*
Turning and turning the bill in the widening gyre,
Decoding the glyphs of the new single:

> *Twenty = single (1993)*
> *E Pluribus Unum = definition of a Po-um*
> *Legal tender = ain't that oxymoronish?*

And then kiss that bill godbye,
Sent off to revitalize the economy,
A salmon arush to spawn
Poetry now informing entire Economy!

The bill folds in on itself
Like the back page of *Mad* magazine
Revealing whole new poem ("New Hole Poem"?),
Can never be
Bought or sold,
Thingless Thing,
Hole poem, as in Poker,

Should not mean
But be poem

So don't be depressed about the state of the world.
Instead be absolutely mournfully depressed! Go ahead,
Be despondent even
Be sad. Being sad is accurate
View of the well of the world
From behind the webbed veil
Of your veiny eyelids.
Gut-wrenching sadness,
Never-to-return-to-any-other-emotion
Sad for insoluble problems be sad
As AIDS cure vomits out of poem, right
As hideous universal inequities are solved by song, sure

Let's all get out of the shower
And sing harmonies and hold hands

Maybe we should put our clothes on first?
Maybe we should rip skins off first!

You shake lion roars:
Grace Utopia Vision Governs Action
Restructures Table of Elements
Now called Elements of Table

As we all sit down. . . .
But who are we? we laugh
Ho ho ha, we are New Poets laughing at ourselves
We are the heroes we've been searching for
We are found in our own backyards,
Right where Dorothy said we'd be

In our own blank, passive potato-face,
The perfect slate on which to scratch this poem

Pierre Revery Interruptus
This just in:
Newsflash Ballot-in
Census Department has decreed
Detailed census of each individual must needs be undertaken
Whitman's huge, he contains multitudes?
Let's count 'em!
Millions of tiny voices freed
Immediately lose track of exact number
Starting over instanter continuously while meanwhile
On to next simile synthesis, here tis:

> *The only contradiction is,*
> *No contradictions!*

As the emergency emerges
Sweet song of poetry must be heard
Petals on a wet black bough
Singing 57
    Gazillion
        Lung-Tongue
           Varieties
               America,
A single bird

FIRE! (Friend or Foe?)

Once
A long long time
Ago

Once upon a time ago
As a matter of fact
Just a second ago
In the beginning
Back to the beginning
Just before the beginning
It was shhh
I'm a-talkin quiet and peace
A riot of quiet
Can you hear it? C'mon try it
You can't hear it? Well that's quiet
Shh Mmmm Bzzz
Didja hear that? In the distance
The insects were buzzing
A language of verbs
& I'm talking
I'm a-talking
I'm a-talking talking bzz-bzz
Little mosquitos
In the ear bzz
Verbosely verbing
Bzzing? Amazing!
Re: "verb"-erating
Suddenly yet subtlely
A luminous lucidity
In the inner inner ear's inner sanctity
The bzz gives way—something's trying to say
The bzz clears
& now you hear

Fire! Fire!—
Fire! (Friend or foe?)

———

A friend (& I use the term advisedly)
A friend once remarked
(Which is rare, in that friends
Usually remark twice—
(Sometimes I think that's the mark of a friend—
The second remark . . .
Sometimes I think that's the mark of a friend—
The . . .))

Fire! Fire!
Fire! (Friend or foe?)

These days with Death so fresh
So deep, so near-at-hand
You feel infected as a Youth
As if there's no Future
That's not polluted
No Past but what's retributed
Nothing to say
Cept "Throw it away!"

Add it to the Great Garbage Heap
Where we sit so gently, my Love
& I, discussing the Forms in the Sky
& like as not, as our toes get toasty
& we look below at the rolly coasty

Lands ablaze like a big gas barbecure
Searing the flesh o' the earth
Well, that's when we start to reflect on
Such as this:

Fire! (we start) Fire! Fire!
Fire! (Friend or foe?)
Fire! (yes, that's how we start) Fire! Fire!
Fire! (Friend or foe?)

Because really we don't know
And as we thus sit thusly
Awaiting the returns of civilization
To answer our small queries
Concerning the Nature of Nature
And Harnessing Destruction and Alternative Alternatives
Until our red hot lips meet
And we make all kinds of passion
Sweet, nasty, hasty, taster,
Flooozy & wicked, bastard prick and
Putting the left-overs in a Tupperware container
Of course because we know nothing lasts forever
Anyway, except nothing lasts forever
Even the thought of Fire, even Fire itself,
Even Fire: Friend or Foe?

The Point

for Luis Rodriguez

The point is
Where we are at
Is the point
Of all returns

We're at the point where you can see clear through

The Crystal Diet Pepsi Lite
Transmogrifying your transcendence
To that point where you prep to the fine
Point the Dinosaur Armor Divisions of the National Guard
While picking your teeth with a grenade handle
Awaiting the verdict on reality itself
As the gates to the Academy of the Future
Are blown
Clear off the hinges
By the implacable forces of the End of History

I used to be a visual aid
Now I'm a hospital

It's all right Ma, I'm only deconstructing

At least the Germans understand
Sandbag the universe
Kill the aliens
Put the kids on drugs
Shave every hair
Hope is a thing called advertising
And poetry my Sweet
Is on MTV

That's right Super Poet
Has devoluted the bod
Into its molecular construct
To pass right through
The lead wall of Plato's *Republic*

The MTVization of Poetry
The Poeticization of MTV

Which gives who gives what gives
A putt putt little motobooty

We rush to rescue something from the burning building
And bring it back into the burning world

Let's unionize the poets
Let's stand up because there are no chairs anyway
Not any real chairs
They are being used to pound a brain with
Some sense at all sense in no sense

It doesn't make it anymore
Sense, I mean, since
Nothing comes over the rainbow
Bob Kaufman's head, smile is a rainbow
It's 1995, you cannot put rainbows in poems anymore!
They've evaporated, become ads,
Madness has been changed into a new breakfast drink
And it's clear
And that's the point

There's a bunch of poets shuffling off to the Slam
Voices are heard, mouths are propellered open and
People have bad breath

The guy who takes my bottles back at the bodega looks so tired
The picture of the smiling Filipino kid on a landfill over
        Jessica Hagedorn's bed

Love comes in the front door without knowing things
The cloak of invisibility is such a great look these days
And a dozen condoms, please, to go

The past is on a rampage
Eating itself
Didumm
Youie hearum abouda veggibles fer eber und
Lizards crawl over the moon, they are not tired,
(No! Not them point!) but wired
Messages coming through at such and such a pace
I'll grab a few deposit slips, an X hat, a kiwi fruit
And hightail it out to the desert where we
Stop dead and pray for clear, cold acid, acid rain

And I am in the Love Canoe

The window is stuck
Howzs the hurricane going to get out

The Crystal Lite Pepsi is boiling over
The Refrogerator Magnets are dangling
I mean dancing
I mean losing pep pop profundity
Poopoohing the poignant and eating bugs raw because
They are haute cuisine bro
Fax machines who said
Fax machines
Fax machines are implanted at birth I am spilling
The delicious venom
The college library is the perfect site
For Transplanted Rain Forest Habitat Salvation Center

Are we there yet
No but we were just there

Is it time yet
Not quite you just passed it
Passed what it
You o'passed the o'point
O'back there o'ways

Notes in your shoes, tacked to genitals
A list to remind yourself to look at the list
The see-through soft drinks with lo-cal alcohol are surfacing
It's so Pure, *Zounds* is making a come back
Because everybody finally knows *Zounds* means
God's Wounds
Bleeding
All over the
Placed point of
Love Caboose! Get the balls,
Get the sapgum! Labia! Labia!
Demagnetized tapes are big smash hits now
Listen to Pure 000
That's right we degauss your brain
You are the auto pilot
Insert a train of yikes thoughts makes no stops
Wherever whenever however whatever
You forgot to express and

What you got left is the point
Of the point
And nuttin but the point
Where something never leads to something else
Because something is
You on the brink of the Great Abyss
And they are quickly extending the overhang

———

Hang on, Sloopy!

Hang on to that point
Oh Gyroscopic Moon,
      balance point of the Wobbling Pivot
Graceful nonpoint gently pushing us back,
Back into the coffin from all directions
Stop me stop me stop me
Before I get to the end

Deacon

for Deacon Lunchbox, 1951–1992

I'm gonna take a walk
Through the carwash tonight
Gonna think my thoughts
Neath the flappin rubber straps

I'm gonna bang my head
On the whirling hoses
Tryin to figure out what
You'd think of this

O! Deacon! It's NY Springtime
Hammerin rushes of sweet Georgia Swingtime

Queer ol' Deacon
In your cigar bra
Catchin fire
In the carwash tonight

The bums found my soul
And it's only a quarter
Queer ol' Deacon
Drying in the water

Creeley's Oral Tradition

Shit, it's
all oral—

when you
hear it you

write it,
when you

read it, you
hear it.

Creeley's Answering Machine

Keep it brief—
can't handle

more than
thirty seconds.

Has There Ever Been Anything BUT Infotainment?!

Purpose of headline is to sell the paper
Purpose of the anchor is to keep you from the zap

Best-seller found in a hotel drawer,
Miracle Man Whomps Apostle Upside Head
Read all about it.

Twixt thumba and afore fing a girl twirls
A tiny globe, we are shaking, which way
Is up anymore! Lugubrious comfort
Who can keep the faith that insists you
Learn History instead of Become It,
A Giant Can opens,

       heartless lover,
Making you quit the job that held it all together
(You equals seam of can, holding can closed.).
The world's foundation is quicksand
And is getting quicker. Out back at Le Brea, it's humans
On exhibition, hyperstacked moments of "Actual

Occurrence" brain pattern display: there, in amber,
La belle Amherst sans merci realizing
That fly buzzing by breaks all news
Like water bag readying birth! Light bulb pops on
On Sir Newton's skull, as grave Apple of Pure Reason
Rumbas air.

Sure, we know Chaucer ripped off Boccaccio,
But that didn't stop Braque and Picassio from cubing
That square, so now everyone can reverse screed
And check all sides simultaneously! Racism

Dies. I marry a hologram.
At midnight the cobbler's shop
Will become the sixth video store

In this town of 5935.
And just yesterday I was complaining
That resoling now costs more
Than buying a brand new pair of shoes.

Talking with a Comet on the Last Day of the Year

Comet blazing overhead, I blink,
Like turn-of-the-century photographer
Slam the plate home. Chemical
Smell, flash powder: off to the side,
Bulb plungered, explosion etches, stretches
Clear to the heavens, here comes Comet
Sliding on down. Ain't no cartoon moonish. No
Belushi. Comet big green cunt prick, switcheroo
Bisex and alien but familiar, if green. (NB:
I think humans are alien, you?)

Except I don't think at all, am falling
Through space much too focused to be
Dream, except maybe much too focused,
The way you are in a dream. "That light
At the end of that tunnel," Comet sings,
"Better hope it ain't no train!" I agree,
Or I think I agree, kind of nodding.

We never know what things mean,
Better far to dream orange apples
In the fridge. I open my
Lover, I open her fan mail, I bake
Bread for her other Lovers and take
The children to a top school.

It's the Last Day
Of God's Advertising Scheme and I wake up
With Comet beside me snoring away as a lush
Aroma swirls. It's the Last Day of the Year
Of the Indecisive Knee Jerk. I'm up late,
Like a copy machine, making little changes,
Subtle respellings, on each copy. "Perhaps
A different vinegar will change your outlook,"
Says Comet, rushing me suddenly from behind,
Pouring what could only be loosely
Called "vinegar" all over me: cold, wet,
Instantly drying. "That's goooood," Comet
Continues, "You be speaking 1992 talk now."
Then the phone rings—has it been ringing
All this time? It's Louisa, saying
She's gotten together with someone.
She sounded so happy I begged her not to stop.

I CAN'T BELIEVE IT'S NOT A POEM!

There's no bidness
In Po-bidness
No bidness
At all!!!!

That's the beauty of Beauty
Not bottled Absolut
In seductive Designer-designed container Container
But pouring gusher freely, absolutely

138

Eureka! I have found it!
And it's Absolutely Everything!

Drilling for purity in the muck
You happen across a little relay
A nugget of meaning is panned out of the Russian River
Formerly the Soviet Union River formerly the Russian River
Grabbing the lever
You settle in for the rest of your days
Right there at the switch
The rest of your days
As in the "sleep" or "nap"
Of your days
Because you rest in a nest of action
You are electric cocoon
Spark molecules explode from you
Tiny words balloon from you
Become crusaders for you
Everything you say steps right up
And shakes hands
Of those with whom
You are speaking
Your commingling conversation
Sets up camp and prepares a good dinner
For twelve strangers invited randomly
Words caressing
Everything swooning
Ei ei o

The great thing about language see
Is when you are just about ready to perform

Triple bypass surgery on the dictionary
You somehow figure out
You don't have to use an IV
Because IV is already in the dictionary
Perhaps you, the Reader
(That is if you are still listening)
Perhaps you, whoever you are, however you got here
I love you. You are thinking
Why does the dictionary need a triple
By now quadruple bypass operation?
BECAUSE MEANING HAS BEEN STRIPPED FROM
      LANGUAGE
BY MEAN-SPIRITED MEANINGLESSNESS MONGERS!
By Greed Blob Blot Demi-humans who wring the Neck of Meaning
As if it were a washcloth, and all we do
Is stand helplessly by as the Liqueur of Understanding
Swirls steadily down the drain
Into the Maw of Moneyitis Midases

What's a bunch of tryin to change the world utopic up's the only
      direction free-spirited teenager poets sposed to do at this
      juncture?
Is there not an alternative, another party perhaps where one can go
to think and play
Rather than drink and bray?
And I, personally, am not talking about such parties as the
Reburplican Dunkeys
      nor Demofrantic Oliphants

What I, personally, am talking about
Is the fact that
I, personally, am

140

PISSED OFF AND MY FRIENDS ARE ALL CRAZY
AND WE, THE SPOKEN WORD SAVAGES, ARE RUNNING
DOWN EVERY STREET IN AMERICA
SHOUTING THE WORDS WHICH YOU NEVER HEAR
YOU ON TELEVISION HORIZONTAL HOLD
MUMBO "I JUST DON'T GET IT" TO
WORDS T-O REVOLUTIONIZE
MESS PLACE USA
!

Words of simple reminder, simply
TO DO SOMETHING BECAUSE WE KNOW INFINITIVE!

We know the "to" part!
We know the t-o "to" part because we are u-p t-o SOMETHING
We are u-p t-o here with the meaningless verbiage
Garbage dreck that has usurped sweet poetry!

So po is dead so we shall bury po
So we shall eat po at special reduced bargain basement rates
And we are the vegetables
Cannibal vegetarian vegetables
Carrots eating carrots with carrots
And onions eating onions with onions

We are motherfucking at harmony with the earth
Beacause we are fatherfucking at war with the destroyers
We are soon to be seen on television
Turning our backs on television
As they roll in the camera with the magic zoom locus
That brings into absolute and horrible focus
The detail of the detail of the detail to choke us
The pseudoquasisemi aggrrrreeeed upon

Single freeze-frame image-reductor image
That has been boiler-plated down from the expansive
Breath life continual zap create reality
That used to be Word
That once was Beauty
The glory that was Po

The powership government has conveniently
Misplaced or forgotten completely
The meaning of t-o govern
The No Think No Thank Tankers refuse to truck in verbs
They think t-o d-o is a noun
And they make a big fuckin to do over it too!
While meanwhile of course
Nothing ever gets done

While meanwhile little boy walks down road
Creating image grapple that image remembers
That road image that
The road seems to be going somewhere
You go too
Follow the image to the allegory
Follow the metaphor to the myth
Here is the dictionary
Here is the noose
And here is the crossroads
The intersection of Dictionary and Noose
Either way you tie
Get all tied up in knots
Except for famous Untie Knot

I give you permission
I am exhilarated as you throw permission back at me

Permission does double back-life goosestep flipoutover—
Permission is rated 10 by the Poetry Slam Dunk Judging
        Commission

I refuse to bunt
I will never slide my hand down the hickory
And half-hunker
To top-spin a slider into an image dying half-way t-o third
As the reader inches around a distant bag
To be moved into so-called scoring position

Because there are too many of because or leads to
The road leads to another road
The land is a map of itself
What is this—the industrialization of the single breath?
Once again, Love steps u-p t-o the plate
The Love Diner is now accepting reservations with an acceptable
        photo-id credit card and a quick phone verification of your
        Emotional Bank Account
Whoops. Sorry buddy, you are overdrawn
At the First National Heart of No Tax Return Insecurity Deposits
        Savings and All Alone

It's not only the only thing
It's not only the thing to do
It's only the only thing to do with the only thing
It's only alone because it's everything
Everything is everything

Deep in the thicket
The purples and blue
Are impenetrable
We are march marching along

On our search for a way
To get out of the way
And you happen across a little relay
A nugget of meaning is panned out of the Russian River
Formerly the Soviet Union River formerly the Russian River

Some people watch snow all night on a box
As poets recycle definitions
The purples and blue
Are impenetrable
As a nugget of meaning

The boy continues down the road merrily
Adding adverbs at every step
Do we follow?

The purples and blue
Are impenetrable

Kill the poets and their lies
But never say kill the poems
Poems never lie

I am a poor wayfarin stranger
A-travelin through this world of woe
Ain't nobody here who can help me
This is the only thing I know

Hey hey hey it's gonna be ok
We got God's cheerleaders on the sidelines
And Emily Dickinson wasn't writin for nuttin

We gotcha papaya salads with iceberg and of course
We got the holes in the Internet
Ei ei o

Did you fall in love yet today?
Dial a number any number spout the love number

Roll over, o mighty whale, and go back to sleep

That's a great last line, Moby:
Roll over, o mighty whale and go to sleep

Where the whale is a metaphor
For all of us
Looking for the rest
Of us
Who haven't been born yet

Let's all take this same deep breath
Let's all take care
As we push a moral dilemma into crowded elevator

I'm looking for a job
While all around there's work that needs to be done

I'm sitting by the side of the long and dusty road
And I cry cry cry
As the television cameras continue to roll

Just me, my jaws quiverin,
Stammerin and yammerin
This is not a poem

Let's Get Butt-Naked and Write Poetry

Gonna tattoo the new to a hot spot
Walk round the sound with a sexy sax—Bought
Ya dreams, soundtrack screams of pleasure
Varieties of touch—a spider's tiny treasure

Sunday afternoon, empty construction zone, a pre-perfect site
To get butt-naked and write the tight
Phat poems that blossom into orbit view
The totale body mesh held by a gold screw

Panoptically watch the goings-on universally
Down below we spy our bodies humping poetry
We're observing love from above
The sweet treat beat
Passionate action friction
Fraction in traction
Watching our bodies grow older never colder—Bolder
In their searching for the depths of each other
Mother father sister brother
The souls of our souls dancing in the ethereal
100% natural material
We're hot rockin the tomb, man
Reinventin man and wo-man

So entwined are we, doubledutching free
Anti-cute in a schoolyard whose verses
Curses and reverses the nurses'
Confessional sign please
To the doctor's obsessional re-re-release
Fingers plying harmonies' delights
Body parts arts signifying hearts

Merciless mercies just lips kissin free
Gettin butt-naked writing poetry

Lean into a concern that'll burn the churn
As the quizzical physical goes astrophysical
With logical magical milestones round yr neck
Neck neck neckin just to hold your head on
No passive observers—just better be gone
We're the same song no one to hear it, come near it
Don't fear it you're in it begin it what's more it
Is just it just when you least expect it
Your being reflects it
Pile on the sweet and tender
Bodies in a blender
Writing poems with skin to the end
Reach the rush   Preach the push
The creative construct comfort input
Anti-compartmentalized as we rise into unity beauty

Till we're all that's left, just each other
One to the other, Sister Brother Lover
"Getting to know you
Getting to know all about you"

Yo
Yo
Yoyo
Yoyo
Love escapes from us
To cover us
Poems us
Surrounded by the sound

Of the meaning of meaning
Dressed up in love so fine
Any meaning mo' yr mine
Stylin, all the while smilin
Walking round the party
In each other's body . . .

And she said:

> Boney maroney ain't no phony
> Tiny hurts blurt the true view
> Vision's revision
> Understand the woman/man difference
> Ain't who wears the pants
> What's growin in me
> Is us and is growin
> In you that's your new tattoo
> In our bed in your head to live life for
> Cry from these kiss these lips to strive for
> Doncha woncha know
> Everybody needs a wife
> Together we'll be the mother
> Not insane, humane—
> Father too
> Me and you
> Delirious serious
> Love grows and grows
> So you must know it
> Grow through, intuit
> Livin through it
> Answer the riddle in the middle:

Let's get butt-naked and write poetry

And write some poetry
Poetry
Uh huh

We Are the Dinosaur

Blast open the gates to kingdom come
Whoops what happened to everyone
Planted a seed—grew into a gun
Dum de dum dum dum dum dum dumb

Life is a riot livin in a cartoon
Ice-age in a dumpster—that's our living room
Set fire to your roof—get a better view
Global warmin is a warnin—toodle-oo

We are the dinosaur
We don't live here anymore
We got what we were askin for
Follow the dinosaur

Ho ho homo sapiens
Ain't so smart
Ka ka kamikaze, Friend
Which way is the ark?

The world is dialin 911
The Don't Walk sign just changed to You Better Run
What we are waiting for has long since come
Dum-de-dum dum dumm dum dum

Cross the scorchin sands with my big fat feet
It's hard becomin diesel fuel with nothin to eat

149

Better catch us quick—we're outta here
We're pre-winged birds & tend to disappear

Hurry, disappear! Back to the Past!
Did you really think the Future was gonna last?
It's endin with a bang so let's have a blast
Let's dine cannibal—it makes a nice contrast

Chauffeured ambulances race to the prom
Santa, please bring me a neutron bomb
Recycle the planet before the earth is a grave
But you must excuse me—gotta get back to my cave

We are the dinosaur
We don't live here anymore
We got what we were askin for
Follow the dinosaur

Relationship

In order to save the relationship
We will never see each other again

Night Fears

Everyone is in love
Except you

Love Poems

I love poems

NOTES

1. Tear To Open (This This This This This This)

To perform the title of "(   )", crook your index fingers and form parentheses on either side of your face, accompanied by a sharp, whistled exhalation. Victor Borge, the Danish lounge comic and classical pianist, pioneered punctuating the air. The title also reflects e e cummings (both his use of punctuations as a character in his poems and his line "death is no parenthesis"). Bill Knott, one of the first "real" poets I ever met, would encase titles in the little arcs, sometimes two sets of parentheses, as if we could never get out, or in. "(   )" is the first of a series of Chinese poems inspired by Prof. Ch'iang Yee, poet/artist/scholar/politician, whose drawings of ideograms on the board at Columbia often evolved into full-blown drawings of gods, landscapes, animals. "(" and ")" are of course reflections themselves, figures on a bridge, the bridge being that which connects. Many of these poems are based on Chinese, interlinear, or translated poems found in *Chinese Poetry* (Yip), *Sunflower Splendor* (Liu and Lo), *Chinese Lyrics* (Ayling and Mackintosh), and others.

"He Refuses to Enter the Marketplace Even to Buy Prestige": *Cafique:* Greek water taxi.

Danny O'Neil was a TV producer who read poetry, a walking oxymoron. When poet/administrator Roberto Bedoya introduced us, he immediately popped the question "Will you help me get poetry on television?" that caused me to reevaluate my dogmatic stance that Poetry and Television being opposites must be at War. Danny died of AIDS before the first "Poetry Spot" appeared on WNYC-TV, a series that has won three Emmys and is now in its sixth season. I am the Producer, as has been Angela Fontanez; shouts to Beni Matias and Jackie Leopold. "Rain" was composed while preparing to mount my bicycle outside Danny's apartment directly across from the Holland Tunnel.

2. Cupid's Cashbox

These poems and others were written on Hydra in the summer of 1985, and published by Jordan Davies in 1989 in a fine press edition including drawings by Elizabeth Murray; some lines are based on writings of Flaubert, Balzac, and Zola. With shouts to Helen and Brice Marden.

3. Beach Simplifies Horizon

A suite of poems comprising a single poem inspired by Cézanne's *Bathers* and his friendship with Zola.

4. Panic*DJ!

*Panic*DJ!* was a performance of poems, raps, and songs that I toured in the '80s, often with musician sidekick Vito Ricci. A PANIC*DJ! performance of your own can be devised by making a selection from these works that integrates "RegPo" and "PerfPo," as Ed Sanders has dubbed regular and performance poetries. Arrange them in a form as comfortable and exciting to the performer as it is entertaining and enlightening to the audience.

"Hey, What'd I Say?" is the slash in a PANIC*DJ! poetry/performance—a poem that literally deconstructs to divide poetry from performance. The poet/performer holds the single sheet on which the poem is written and tears off each line or section as it is read, rotating the page clockwise, tearing as you go, holding onto the shreds, until only the "center" verse (beginning "The words themselves!") remains. After the last line ("O air! Carry them/to ears that hear!") is read, toss the scraps into the air so that they flutter down, ending the poem, and leaving the poet empty-handed to carry on by heart. The poem was begun under the influence of Jessica Hagedorn, great poet and performer and novelist, in her days as leader of the Gangster Choir.

"SWEAT&SEX&POLITICS!" Rap with music by Vito Ricci. Cassette version also has Kenny Aaronson on bass and Johnny Mann on DMX. A slightly different version of this rap was used for the Manhattan Poetry Video Project's "RAPP IT UP!" produced by Rose Lesniak, which, along with poems by Allen Ginsberg and Anne Waldman, are the first ever poetry videos. "S&S&P!" was a big hit in Managua, as translated by Amparo Leon. "Thought is made in the mouth"—Tristan Tzara. Title courtesy of friend and artist Lori Landes.

"Beside Myself" was performed with Kenneth King and Dancers at LaMama, in 1982. William Tudor composed a musical setting for this poem.

"Cellular Phone": Commissioned by the producer Ed Goodgold, whose concept for a new band with a Sade-sound and actual product-mentions in the lyrics yielded DYFM (Designer Yuppie Fuck Music). Music by Vito.

"Zooin' in Alphabet Town": Composed while on a walking tour of Loisaida with "Da Mayor of Harlem," Hendrix biographer, poet, and friend David Henderson. We were In Search Of . . . Images! David would run down the street and shout, There's one! and I'd write it down. Written in early '80s when Avenue A *was* the DMZ, gentrification just beginning to dent the Lower East Side.

"Recipe": Edwin Denby casually mentioned that the shape of some new poems looked like recipes. This poem was his dessert.

"THE IMPOSSIBLE RAP": I told Vito Ricci I wanted to write a rap about how fascism began at home, how you can't think any thought but the thought you're thinking, how I wanted to write in the voice of The Other Thought. Vito's reply: That's impossible.

"The Proposal": Epithalamium for Stuart Hanlon and Kathy Ryan.

"Night": Under Sandino's sombrero reading Ruben Dario's *Azul*. In Nicaragua, poetry is second only to baseball as national pastime.

"The Meaning of Meaning": Begins with the performer not knowing what piece this is ("I don't have any idea . . ."), and asking the musical accomplice to fill in the blanks of this first Metaphysical Pop tune.

"I'd Rather Be Crazy Than Stupid": Music by Stuart Holman. Performed with taped brother Stu on guitar, bass, and back-up vocals as ghetto blaster is cradled in performer's arms.

"ROCK'N'ROLL MYTHOLOGY" was released as a single in 1981 by Words on 45, b/w "Made in Japan" by Ann Rower; music on both cuts by Vito Ricci. Voices on the rap are triple-tracked, so in performance PANIC gets to have a trialogue with himself. As performed with dancer Yoshiko Chuma and the School of Hard Knocks, "R'N'R Myth" takes on truly mythic proportions as a call-and-response rap, an idea suggested by Ron Padgett. The opening sections have appeared in "Words in Your Face" and on the first MTV "Spoken Word Unplugged."

5. Volume Dips and Variable Speeds:
From Steve Cannon's Stoop to the Mithraic Podium

Professor Steve Cannon is el Faro del Loisaida, the Lighthouse of the Low East, an inspiration to generations of poets in that neighborhood. Poet, playwright, and retired professor from Medgar Evers College, he is also the Only Paid Heckler in New York City, with an Endowed Chair at the end of the bar at the Nuyorican Poets Café. When Steve and I noticed that poets were slamming with the same poem over and over, never lifting it from some raggedy notebook, actually becoming known for writing these one or two crowd-pleasers, it was time to acknowledge that the pendulum had swung too far—we were being bushwhacked by the Café's success. Performance had swept text out with the dust that had been the boring poems. So began "The Stoop," a weekly gathering preceding the Slams, where poems were shredded, research and reading required, and where textual parallels of the oral tradition began to show through. The actual Stoop, outside 285 East Third Street, leads to Steve's Tribes Gallery, which always has an art show on exhibition and is the editorial office for the top-of-the-line cultural magazine *A Gathering of the Tribes* he publishes. Steve has also been known to physically sit on the Stoop and observe all that goes on in his blindness, occasionally letting loose with his Heckler's Chant: *"Read the fuckin' poem!"*

153

Mithras was the Bull God who directly preceded Christianity in Rome—you can find Christian churches that simply redecorated Mithraic temples when they switched over to Jesus. In the cellar of one such church, San Clemente, is a magnificent stone-carved podium, ready for a poetry reading, Slam, and Open Room. I am working on reading *The Collect Calls of the Wild* there: "No bull" as Basil Bunting says in the Jonathan Williams photo.

"Censor Not": In performance, remember to censor the "c" in censor!

"Etruscan Suns"–"No Dream": These poems were written Spring 1991, while Elizabeth and I were in residence at the American Academy in Rome, to which: Gratitude.

"Good to Hear from You": Gregory Kolovakos, while Director of the Literature Program of the New York State Council of the Arts, activated that institution to become a force instead of a tablecloth. When he toured the wrecked building that would reopen as the Café in 1989, he was enthusiastic but realistic—told me to give it two years and if it wasn't happening, move on, this being the time of grant slashes with censorship battles on the horizon. Gregory died of AIDS the next year, but his spirit pushes the Café to this day. An exquisite translator, mover and shaker. This poem was written at his memorial.

"Poetry Balance Balances Life Off the Speakers" is for that moment of stasis when Bimbo Rivas, poet hero and originator of the term Loisaida, forgot the next line of the poem and had to reinvent himself to complete the couplet. He and I thus once raged a poetry throwdown at Irma Alagarín's. Death by heart attack while reciting before a kindergarten class in 1992. Visit his mural on C ("Loisaida Avenue") between Fourth and Fifth. In performance: Balance the titles, balance the poet and poem, receive the balance of wobbling pivot and Bimbo ever-spinning.

"The Irony of the Ecstasy": It was at Miky Piñero's Wake and Wake-up Call at Roland Legiardi-Laura's loft, following the Scattering of the Ashes over the Lower East Side, that I urged everyone to tell Miguel Algarín that it was time to reopen the Café. Understand that the building was a shambles at this point, and the quest to reopen had been unsuccessfully attempted several times previously. I was worn down by trying to shake my Plain White Rapper's ass into public view and was ready to settle down into a space; Miky's passing brought us all together. And that was the way it was as we spent a year focusing on the adventure in poetry that forms without institutionalizing. Miguel, who is the Mayor of the Block, often had young kids sit in his car to look out for Brownies (NYC Parking Violations Bureau officers)—Cecilio had just graduated to actual driver. It was while running down Canal Street with a gas can that I had the vision of reentering Plato's *Republic*, from which poets had been banished for three thousand years.

"Underdose o' Café": Pre-Slam at the Café, during the "DisClaimer," it is always announced that you may write on bar napkins poems composed of fragments of the poems you hear, and thus become a poet yourself and read said poem at the Open Room, begun by the Café's True Hero, Lois Griffith, and continuing to this day hosted by Café Classico, Keith Roach. And what would a book be without the inclusion of just such a poem, written in the twilight zone of consciousness.

"La Petite Punaise . . ." was written as birth announcement for Sophia Murray Holman, 12/26/82. The title was clucked to her on her second day by a nurse at Beth Israel.

"Little Dipper" was written as birth announcement for Daisy Sally Murray Holman, 4/30/85. It is written in the Reverse Half-Sonnet (Waa! aaw!) form.

"Birthday Morning, 1991": It was Elizabeth's birthday, but that didn't stop Sophie's rock'n'roll chicken alarm clock from awaking the family.

"My TV Poem": Written with Daisy Holman.

"No Longer Killing Mosquitos": Thanks to Joe Flaherty, Todd Beers, and Writers and Books in Rochester, N.Y., for the Residency, and Down With Jeff McDaniel, who made me explain myself.

"A tiny flash . . ." was written for Butch Morris's "Poets Chorus" at the Stoop. Performed at the Whitney Midtown and the Public Theater.

6. I Can't Believe It's Not a Poem!

Many things are not poems, but everything can be. If Zukofsky were to give his test (see his *A Test for Poetry*), today's question might start with "Is THAT a poem?" asked specifically for each so-called poem in this book. Asking that question (as in Creeley's essay, "Is That a Real Poem or Did You Just Make It Up Yourself?") begins engagement in the contact sport that is poetry. This section includes my most recent writings.

I clipped the notice from the *Village Voice* "Choices": Panel discussion at the 92nd Street Y regarding "The Future of Poetry"—What? Who? All the participants were tenured professors who thought the Future of Poetry was pretty bleak because many M.F.A. writing programs were cutting back on their faculty positions. WAKE UP! shouted Mike Tyler, Edwin Torres, and other Café poets who had ventured uptown, Poetry is exploding a different Future! Becoming part of the world again, entering your livingrooms via television, Slamming across the country on Internet! "The Death of Poetry"?—I can't believe it's not a poem!

"1990" premiered at PANIC*DJ!'s final performance at the Great Hall of Cooper Union. Here, where Lincoln and Twain had Chattaquaed, Vito Ricci took a break from playing as I soloed this straight poem and realized that my work in defining

"Rap is poetry"—in using musical accompaniment to set a poem familiarly into the ear—had ended. The new music is no music. There is nothing so radical as the words themselves, careening meaning.

"DisClaimer": Pedro Pietri and I began working together as CETA poets in the late '70s. In the '80s we began our "The Double Talk Show: The only late-nite TV show not on TV" and "Poets in the Bars: A Celebration of the Oral Tradition" at literary watering holes across town. His brother, Dr. Willie, was always a guiding spirit. Shouts to Carmen, Joe, Frank, from Bob Pietri.

The Green Mill Tavern is an exquisite sight, a jazz bar with roots as a Capone-era speakeasy. Marc Smith, poet, Slam progenitor, former construction worker, was out of commission when I attended my first Slam there in 1988. Years later I would interview Marc and learn that he was laid up at the time, having been involved in a car crash and bashed by punks on the way home from the Mill, and had undergone an Epiphany in the hospital: To dedicate himself to poetry, to Slam, to audience control of art.

There are currently Slams in over thirty cities across the country. These mock Olympics of poetry are all independently run, organized by poets, and vary drastically in tone, but all have some method of judging, usually by individuals selected whimsically from the audience, with "I've never been here before and don't know how to do it" being a great qualification. In general, judges rate the poems from 0, a poem that should never have been written, to 10, a poem achieving simultaneous orgasm throughout the entire audience. It cannot be denied that a poet once received a score of minus infinity, nor that judges are urged to use the finer points of the Dewey Decimal Slam System to both heighten the ironies and lessen the chance for ties, which result in the Dreaded Sudden Death Haiku Overtime Rounds. The purpose being to hear poetries aloud, to come into contact with literature as part of life, and to hear that poetry comes in as many styles as music does, who is speaking to you?

In "What You Can't Understand Is Poetry Is Connected to the Body Again," "Jean" was inspired by Jean Howard, who, along with Kurt Heintz and Michael Warr, runs the Chicago Poetry Video Festival. Yes, that is Emily Dickinson's fly!

"Head of Kovacs" was commissioned by TV producer and friend Diggins, who had to create opening titles at the head of the Kovacs shows which were to be run on cable. As far as I know, Percy Dovetonsils was the first poet to appear on national television.

In the midst of the battle to proclaim the many influences of the new poets at the Café and other sites (the Beats being only one important strand among many influ-

156

ential poetries), I was invited to participate in a Neal Cassady reading. And lo, I was visited by the spirit of Neal, who spoke of Lew Welch, the Beat poet who disappeared into the desert, and other matters.

"57 Gazillion Lung-Tongue Varieties" takes its title from a version of Mayakovsky's "Mystery Bouffe" I wrote for the Shaliko Theater Company. Bob Carroll, an itinerant writer and performer, was a total inspiration for the activation and possibilities of art. His "Salmon Show" managed to illustrate the U.S. economy through the life cycle of a salmon, which Bob somehow proclaimed with one hand while balanced on one leg and offering audience members a beer or seltzer with the other. He died of AIDS in 1987. Emily XYZ is a Nuyorican Poets Café denizen, a poet who often writes dual-voiced performance pieces. Pierre Reverdy was a French Surrealist poet of the early 1900s.

"FIRE! (Friend or Foe?)" takes as its start the friendly-fire deaths in the Gulf War, and deep image: AIDS. Performed as a rap, with music by Vito Ricci, who also wrote music for "We Are the Dinosaur."

"The Point" began as a letter to Luis Rodriguez, friend and poetry activist. Luis and I have done gigs together from "Chicken's Road House" in southeastern Ohio to snazzy restaurants in LA; we've been on panels together and hung out at Seattle's Bumbershoot, thanks to Judith Roche. He's a battler for the power of the word, his Tia Chucha Press and activities with gangs and homeless people make him a model for the poet of the next millennia. I vote for Luis, who's the author of *Always Running.*

"Deacon": Lunchbox, poet laureate of Atlanta, was a star of "Words in Your Face," directed by Mark Pellington, produced by Josh Blum and me, for PBS's "Alive TV." Deacon died in a rock'n'roll car crash in 1992.

How come nobody else thinks Robert Creeley is a performance poet? I didn't get his work at all till I hitchhiked to Swarthmore College in the late '60s to hear him read: as he etched the words in air, I saw sound. The emotion couldn't stay stuck in his throat, and when I met Ted Berrigan, the way poets learn ear-to-ear came into focus.

"Has There Ever Been Anything BUT Infotainment?!": The "best-seller" referred to is of course the Bible; Poet Laureate Joseph Brodsky recommended placing poetry anthologies alongside the Gideon Bibles, saying that the Bible could handle the competition, a feat now being accomplished by Andrew Carroll and the American Poetry Literacy Project. La belle Amherst is Emily Dickinson somehow appearing in Andrew Marvell's poem, "La Belle Dame Sans Merci." As I hear it, *The Canterbury Tales* were sampled from *The Decameron,* which is no excuse for rhyming Boccaccio and Picassio,

157

but Cubism is. 5935 is the population of combined Town and Village of Granville, New York, the Colored Slate Capital of the World, as of the 1990 census.

"I CAN'T BELIEVE IT'S NOT A POEM!" was written for New York poet Eileen Myles's race for the Presidency in 1992.

> My life is the poem I would have writ
> But I could not both live and utter it.
> —Thoreau